THE GREEN ELEVATOR CAGE

CLAUDE RAKISITS

This edition first published in paperback by
Michael Terence Publishing in 2024
www.mtp.agency

Copyright © 2024 Claude Rakisits

Claude Rakisits has asserted the right to be identified as
the author of this work in accordance with the
Copyright, Designs and Patents Act 1988

ISBN 9781800948655

This is a work of fiction. Unless otherwise indicated,
all the names, characters, businesses, places, events and
incidents in this book are either the product of the author's imagination
or used in a fictitious manner. Any resemblance to actual persons,
living or dead, or actual events is purely coincidental

No part of this publication may be reproduced, stored
in a retrieval system, or transmitted, in any form or
by any means, electronic, mechanical, photocopying,
recording or otherwise, without the prior
permission of the publisher

Cover design (AI)
Michael Terence Publishing

Michael Terence
Publishing

"Secrets are lies by another name."
Michael Morpurgo

To my grandmother and mother...

Prologue
(1963)

I moisten the transparent stamp hinge with a small yellow sponge and stick it on the back of the stamp. I then place it on the look-alike image of the stamp. And there it is my very first stamp in this very thick stamp album. It's an Australian stamp of a British king, George VI, I think. In any case, I'm proud of it. It looks old, which it is, and it looks valuable, which it isn't, otherwise I wouldn't have it. I also have many stamps of the British queen, Elizabeth II. She's just about on every Australian stamp, as well as on the stamps of many other countries. She must be an important person.

Uncle Pierre has just bought me this stamp album for my seventh birthday, and I'm keen to fill it. It's like doing a jigsaw puzzle. I'm lucky because I have a steady supply of stamps thanks to Mum's many postcards from exotic lands and faraway places I've never heard of. I know it'll take me a long time to fill that stamp album, not only to find all those stamps but also to put them into the album. But I have plenty of time. I have my whole life to complete this project.

I can't wait to show my stamp album to Claudia.

1

Canberra – The Phone Call (2000)

The phone rang, ripping the tranquillity of the night air into the before and the after. The radio clock, with its blood-red numbers, screamed 3:12 am.

Max, having just returned to bed after putting Genevieve back to sleep, answered the phone quickly so that Jane wouldn't be woken up. She was an even worse sleeper than their two-year-old daughter.

'Hello?'

Silence.

'That's okay, Mum. What's wrong?'

Silence.

'Oh no. When?'

Silence.

Jane had woken up and was already comforting Max, kissing him on the arm.

'...Yes, I'm still here,' he said, having real difficulties continuing the conversation.

Silence.

'Did she suffer much?'

Silence.

'...Mum, can I call you back in a bit? It's very early here and I'm really sad,' Max tried to say between deep sobs.

Silence.

'Thank you, Mum, and how are you going?'

Silence.

'…You're right. She had a very good life. Ninety-seven is pretty good.'

Silence.

'I'll call you back in a couple of hours. I love you.'

'I'm so sorry, darling. I know how close you were to her, what she meant to you,' Jane said to Max as she cuddled him and patted his back.

'Thank you, sweetheart.' Max cried deeply, repeatedly wiping his tears with the back of his hand. 'She was so much to me. So much. You can't imagine. She was my mother when my mother was having a good time flying around the world, leaving me behind. It's so sad. So sad.' He kept thinking of that green elevator cage.

2

Canberra – Reflections (2000)

A couple of days after his mother had called him to break the devastating news of his grandmother's death, Max poured himself a glass of white wine, put on Pergolesi's Stabat Mater, probably his favourite classical CD, and went to the first-floor veranda at the front of the house. He loved that space, especially in the evenings when the light would begin to dim, and the night slowly embraced the native garden. He could then savour the scores of plants he had nurtured over the years and admire the beautiful Australian birds munching away on the seeds in the birdfeeder he had built. Here he could simply contemplate life and relax. It was paradise.

He thought of Mammy, his grandmother. He could still remember when he had gone to Brussels to visit her before coming to Australia in 1982. He had just spent six years in Vancouver, where he had done his undergraduate and master's degrees. He had loved living in Canada and had intended to stay, but Sophie, his girlfriend of over five years, abruptly ended the relationship. He still didn't understand why, and probably never would. She didn't want to discuss it. She had decided that it was over, and that was that. No explanation. He did have his suspicions that she may have gone off with her lab partner. What he did know was that he was utterly crushed by the experience. His youth and his utter love for her had

The Green Elevator Cage

blinded him to that thunderbolt out of nowhere. He eventually got over the broken heart, as does everyone. In any case, she had done him a favour. Instead, he came to Australia, married a beautiful woman and together they had a gorgeous child. A pretty good ending to a very sad story, he thought.

He took a sip of his wine.

The resident magpie landed on the railing and looked at him. They knew each other well. Max always gave him worms or grubs from the garden whenever he was gardening, which was often. Once he saw he had nothing to offer this evening he flew away.

He knew back then in 1982 that he wouldn't be seeing much of Mammy in the future. And he had been right. He only saw her three times, very briefly, each time on the way to an academic conference. He now deeply regretted it, especially after all she had done for him over the years. He had been selfish, and he knew it.

He took another sip of his wine.

His daughter came wobbling over onto the veranda. She looked at him. 'Oh Daddy, you crying!' as she pointed her little index finger to his tears silently running down his cheeks.

'It's okay my sweet pea. I'm fine,' smiling.

He picked her up and sat her on his lap. 'Je t'adore, Genevieve.'

'I love you too, Daddy,' as she gave him a big kiss on the cheek and hugged him.

'Go and get me a Tintin book and I'll read it to you.'

She smiled with pleasure. 'Oui, Papa.' She jumped off his lap and ran off to her bedroom.

But Australia hadn't always been plain sailing.

Soon after arriving in Brisbane to do his PhD at the University of Queensland, he met Anne who was doing a master's in political development in the South Pacific. He immediately fell in love with her. He adored her light-blue eyes and before he knew it, they were in a relationship. Within months they were living together. She helped him get over Sophie. He remembered that he loved her, but he also knew that it wasn't passionate love, the sort that makes you unable to eat or sleep. Still, she helped him deal with the utterly dysfunctional nature of the department of political science, where everyone fought each other, most did little work and all probably drank too much. The university pub was effectively the head of the department's main office. As for his PhD supervisor, a grumpy German bachelor, could at times be difficult, but, overall, was decent. All in all, those were happy days with Anne.

Max took a sip of his wine.

A large sulphur-crested cockatoo landed on the veranda railing and stared at him, with his head cocked sideways so he could have a better look at him. But he flew away when Jane came onto the veranda. She bent over to give Max a soft kiss on the lips.

Caressing his shoulder, 'How are you bearing up, darling?'

'I'm fine, darling. Just thinking about Mammy, the past, my mother, everything all jumbled up. All very sad really.'

'I understand. It's normal.'

'I know. But you are never really ready for it.'

'She had a full life. And I also know that you brought her a lot of happiness.'

'Probably also a lot of angst during the teenage years.'

Jane crouched down next to Max. She put her hand on his, squeezed it and caressed it. He loved her red fingernails. Always did.

'Darling, this was never going to be easy. I know how much she meant to you.'

'Thank you so much for your support.'

'Oh darling, of course.'

'If it's okay with you, I'm thinking of going to the funeral.'

'Of course, I expected you to.'

'Thank you. I won't be gone very long.'

'Take whatever time you need. It's a chance to see family members.'

He looked at her. 'Thank you.'

'Can I get you another glass of wine?'

'Yes, that would be nice. And could you put on "Kind of Blue"?'

'Done!'

Max went back to his reverie. He started wondering when the relationship with Anne started to go sour. He thought it was her father's dogmatic insistence that if they got married it had to be a Catholic wedding. Nothing else would do. Although the father was a third-generation Australian, his Catholic Irish roots were still very much part of his DNA. Hardwired. As someone who had been brought up as a Catholic and had gone to a Catholic boarding school in Belgium, Max should have been comfortable with that, but his relationship with God had never been a close one. So, he felt he would be lying to himself, and the congregation were he to go ahead with such a wedding. Anne sided with her authoritarian father.

But the bottom line, the real bottom line, was that he wasn't ready to get married, certainly not to Anne. And she knew it. So, they parted amicably, without too much fuss, or with too many tears. Still, it was a sad, but not a totally unexpected ending to a beautiful relationship. He would always be grateful to her for enabling him to stay permanently in Australia. They sometimes bumped into each other in Canberra and would have a bit of a chat, but that caravan had moved on.

The evening was fast settling in. The birds had tucked in for the night.

Jane came back with his glass of wine.

'Thank you, darling. Where is Genevieve?'

'She's playing in her room. I'm about to feed her.'

'She must have been distracted because she was going to come back with a Tintin book for me to read to her.'

'You can read it to her when she goes to bed.'

'Yes, of course.'

'I'm going to start cooking us dinner.'

'Can I help?'

'No, just stay put. You need some quiet time.' She bent down and kissed him on the lips. 'I love you.'

'I love you so much too.'

Max took a sip of his wine. It was now completely dark. He lit a candle that was on the wrought-iron table in front of him. It flickered peacefully, dancing slightly to the warm breeze. It was mesmerizing.

He would never forget the day he bumped into Jane. It felt like yesterday. It was not that long after breaking up with Anne. He happened to be shopping at the local farmers' market in Canberra sometime in 1993. He remembered distinctly that as he was reaching out to pick

The Green Elevator Cage

a tomato, a woman's hand, with beautiful fingernails painted with red nail polish, reached out for the very same tomato. Their hands touched. He looked over to his left to see who owned that beautiful hand. And there was Jane. He hadn't seen her since his field trip to Pakistan some ten years earlier. He remembered her well. She was at the time the third secretary at the Australian High Commission in Islamabad. He had seen her a few times during his six-month field trip. What impressed him most was that she always wore the most attractive red lipstick, which was always colour-coordinated with her fingernail polish. Very classy, he thought.

He took a sip of his wine.

Things moved quickly. This time Max knew she was the one. They were married within three years. It was a beautiful civil wedding, with just the right number of people. Sadly, no one from Max's family came. No one. He didn't think it was anything malicious, it was just that they didn't seem to care. Quite frankly, he was rather indifferent. After moving to Australia, the already tenuous family ties weakened even more. Jane, on the other hand, was shocked, as was her family. But then, Max thought, given his family history and the long bouts of separation, it wasn't surprising, not at all. Boarding school and Canada hadn't helped things.

'Dinner is ready, darling,' Jane called out.

'I'll be right there.'

He got up and blew out the candle.

3

Brussels – The Game of Monopoly (1958-1964)

'Ils ont tué Lumumba. Ils ont tué Lumumba.'[1]

I would have been about six when I kept repeating those words about the assassination of Patrice Lumumba, the first prime minister of the newly independent Democratic Republic of the Congo, the former Belgian Congo.

'You must stop saying this, Michel!' Uncle Pierre scolded me each time, with a raised voice. But I'd ignore him. I just loved the word Lumumba; it rolled off the tongue so easily.

Running off in front of Uncle Pierre, I yet again repeated, 'Ils ont tué Lumumba.'

No one in Brussel's Park Elisabeth seemed to be surprised by my utterance. On the contrary, most people smiled, approvingly. In Belgium, everyone knew who Lumumba was. He was the Congolese chap who had humiliated Belgian King Baudouin during the hand-over celebrations in Leopoldville six months earlier.

I don't think I knew then that I was born in Leopoldville in 1956, four years before independence. The only thing I knew was that Lumumba was what Uncle

---

[1] "They've killed Lumumba"

Pierre and my grandmother, Mammy, talked a lot about around the kitchen table.

****

Today was a big day. My mother was coming to visit. She was an airline stewardess, so she was back from one of her many trips to exotic lands, to places that all sounded so fantastic. I was so excited. I told my yellow canary, which lived in a small cage in the kitchen, that my mother would be coming today. He responded by jumping back and forth from one perch to the only other one, chirping away. He too was excited. I had had him ever since I could remember. Every morning after getting out of bed I'd go straight to the kitchen to see him. And he'd welcome me with his beautiful song. I treasured him.

I also told my canary that my mother was the most beautiful woman in the world. I'd say the same to Mammy as we watched the television together in the evenings. When a female announcer would start talking, I'd turn to my grandmother and say, 'She thinks she's beautiful but she's nothing next to my beautiful mother.' And Mammy would turn to me, hold my hand tenderly and say, 'I know, Michel darling.'

On this visit, my mother brought me a soft brown teddy bear straight from a place called Alaska. I loved the teddy bear right away. It didn't really matter what my mother brought me. Whatever she brought I automatically cherished. That night I fell asleep with it, clutching it for dear life.

'Were you a good boy while I was away?' my mother asked me, as she would each time she came back to visit. I always said yes, and each time she would say the same thing to me, 'I know you would be because you're the best little boy in the world.' I was so happy each time she said that to me.

We all went to the park that day and I rode my bicycle which had training wheels. I sped ahead of them to show them how fast I could go on my bicycle. We stopped by the ice cream van and, as always, I got an ice cream cone with two balls of vanilla, my favourite flavour. The ice cream man was such a nice man. He always knew what I was going to ask for. My world was complete: I had my beautiful mother, my loving Mammy and Uncle Pierre. What more could a six-year-old boy ask for?

But as always, this happiness would end too soon. My mother would leave me once again for exotic lands. I know because she would send me postcards with beautiful stamps from around the world. I so much looked forward to getting them. I knew they were from her because the writing, always in green ink, looked like stick figures playing on the card.

The day she left, she was wearing a gorgeous, colourful dress, as women did in those days. Her hair was up in a chignon, she wore bright red lipstick, and her long white gloves were so soft to the touch. I loved her dearly.

'I will be back very soon darling, I promise,' she said. 'So, don't be sad, Mammy will take very good care of you.' But I couldn't help it. It was asking too much from a six-year-old not to be sad to see his mother leave him, once again. I only wanted her to stay with me. That's all. I cried with so much pain, with tears dripping down my cheeks, begging her not to leave me, reaching out as Mammy was holding me back, to please stay only one more day. That's all, only one more day.

The Green Elevator Cage

But to no avail, after one last warm kiss on the cheek, and the softest touch of her gloved-hand on my cheek to wipe my tears, she stepped into the small, green elevator, which could only take four people, drew the accordion-like door and pressed the button. And she was gone, once again.

****

'Who's this?' I asked Mammy, as I pointed to a black and white picture in the photo album of a man wearing khaki shorts, long socks and a pith helmet. Two Africans were standing uncomfortably a certain distance from the white man in the picture. 'This is your grandfather, Bonpa, in the Belgian Congo in the 1940s,' she replied. 'He loved Africa so much. The Congolese who worked with him liked him a lot. He was good to them. But I never felt comfortable there. It was so different from Belgium. The natives scared me.'

Mammy turned the pages of the photo album, commenting on some of the pictures and sometimes saying nothing. I loved those moments together when she would tell me stories as we looked at those small, fading black-and-white pictures with jagged edges. We were sitting in the kitchen next to each other at the plastic-covered table with flowers as a motif. I was drinking a cup of hot cocoa, and my grandmother had a cup of coffee. My canary was chirping away in the background.

'And who is this girl?' I asked. 'She's beautiful,' pointing to an adolescent girl wearing a summer dress.

'That's your mother in the Congo when she was 15. Everyone loved her so much. She was also very good in school. She came first in French even though she hardly spoke any French, only Flemish when we arrived in Leopoldville in 1946.'

'Who's that?' pointing to a boy.

'That's Uncle Pierre, he was only a little boy then. But I was always worried that someone would try to kidnap him, and I would never see him again.'

Turning the page, I pointed to a picture of a girl looking over a baby in a crib and touching its cheek. 'Who's that?'

'That's you in the Congo. You were only a couple of months old there. That's where you were born. And that's Claudia, your sister.'

'What?! I have a sister?' looking up to Mammy, totally shocked. I stared at the picture. 'How old is she?'

'She's three years older than you, she's ten. But it's best your Mum tells you about Claudia,' she said. 'Anyway, I have to start dinner,' as she took away the photo album and put it on top of the bookshelf where I couldn't reach it.

That evening, I went to bed thinking about Claudia, wondering what she looked like and why she wasn't with me. I fell asleep thinking of us playing hide and seek in the park.

****

Taking the bus to Hingene, my grandmother's native village in Flanders, was always an adventure. I loved the long ride and the many stops in all the small towns on the way. Even though it wasn't actually that far it still took well over an hour to get there. That was an eternity for a little boy. There was so much to look at through the window.

The Green Elevator Cage

I would rush into the bus, run up the aisle and pick a row. I would look back to have Mammy's approval before sliding across the green vinyl bench to sit by the window. As a little boy, with my feet not touching the floor, I would easily slip forward. But Mammy was there to hold me so that I was secure next to her. We always sat to the right of the driver so that we had a better view of where we were going.

Even though it was exciting to look out of the window, it could get a bit boring, so I always brought with me the latest edition of 'Spirou', my favourite weekly comic magazine. Uncle Pierre and I would buy it every Thursday, which was the day it came out. I so much looked forward to the day because I would be able to read the rest of the serialised stories. One of my favourite ones was the one of Sandy and his pet kangaroo. This was the first time I'd heard of Australia. It seemed like a very exciting place to live. Sandy was always doing adventurous things with his kangaroo. He lived on a very large property far away from everywhere else. His father raised sheep and cattle. I always thought that I should go there one day to visit.

We were always met at the bus stop in Hingene by Mouke, Mammy's mother, my great-grandmother. She was very old, and she only wore black; her husband having died fifty years earlier. She only had one tooth left, the top one, like a baby. We'd walk back to her place, most of it along a poplar-lined canal populated with ducks.

I liked my great-grandmother a lot. I used to play card games with her, and I used to ruthlessly cheat. I never liked to lose, I still don't. And if it meant I had to cheat to win against Great-Granny, so be it. She suspected strongly that I was cheating, so she would tell my grandmother. But Mammy dismissed that accusation, claiming that I was an angel and that I would never do such a thing. I liked that line and so I continued to cheat whenever I played with Mouke.

Mouke's home, which was part of a small farm, was very small, with only two rooms, and it was always dark, damp and cold. It was only later that I realised that it was, sadly, at best a hovel. In the front room, which was a kitchen, living room and dining room, all combined in one, there was a coal-heated stove which did break the chill a bit, but not much. There was a small rug on the rough wooden floor in front of the used green armchair and the very old, small couch for two. The lighting was poor, with only an overhead, low-wattage ceiling light and a free-standing reading light which also provided very little light. The walls were to all intents and purposes, barren. There was the ubiquitous wooden cross with a figure of a dying Jesus above the stove, with a dried Palm Sunday leaf stuck in the back. The only other thing on the wall was a black and white, very faded photograph of a family picture of a much younger Mouke with her late husband and their five children. The picture was so old I wasn't even able to recognise Mammy. There was no television; there was no radio. It was a very boring place for a seven-year-old!

I can trace the origin of my uneasiness with dogs to my visits to Hingene. Across from Mouke's home, which was on one side of a wide courtyard, there was a large, black German Shepherd locked up behind a wire mesh. The dog, which was tied up to a long, heavy chain, barked loudly and snarled deeply, showing his sharp teeth with saliva drooling from his muzzle as he leapt from one end of his enclosure to the other. He looked very angry, vicious and positively dangerous. He scared me enormously. And even though he was locked up in a cage, I always feared that he would manage to gnaw his way through the metal grill, come after me and savagely rip me apart in the dead of night. I have never forgotten that dog.

I never forgot the day Mouke was buried. Her son, Joseph, who was the local gravedigger, had personally dug his mother's burial pit. I was holding Mammy's hand, standing along with everyone else as the coffin was being lowered slowly into the ground. And then one of the attendants lowering the coffin with the ropes slipped and the coffin fell on its side at the bottom with a loud thud. Everyone gasped in horror. Joseph had to jump into the pit to fix the problem. It was a scene of utter mayhem and confusion.

****

Like everyone else in Belgium on 1 November, All Saints Day, I used to go with Mammy to the tomb of my grandfather, Bonpa, her husband, who was buried in a cemetery in Bruges, to lay chrysanthemums. Bonpa had died from lung cancer about a year before I was born. He was only 51. As we stood there holding hands looking at the tomb, having placed the flowers, I used to think that it would have to be very lonely there for him under that very heavy slab of marble. There was a small picture of him, the same as the one of him in the living room, embedded in the headstone. He was wearing a uniform, with lots of medals on his chest. Mammy regularly told me that he was one of the most decorated men in Belgium.

Those same medals were in a framed, glass box on the wall next to my bed. At night, lying in bed, I would look at those medals and fall asleep very sad, sometimes crying, thinking how he must have suffered to earn all those medals.

****

Today was another big day; Mammy had told me that Mum was going to be with us for a few days. I'd wait for her by the green elevator just outside our front door on the landing. I'd wait to hear the sound of the elevator begin to come up. Sadly, not each time the elevator ascended was it coming to the fourth floor, the top floor. But once I knew the lift was coming to our floor, then I knew that I would very soon be hugging my mother. She hardly had time to get out of the lift and I had already leapt into her arms, hugging her for dear life, drowning her with a million kisses. I was in heaven.

One day, while I was sitting in the kitchen with Mum, Mammy and Uncle Pierre, I asked Mum if we could look at the photo album. I'd been waiting for this day for a long time.

'Of course, we can Michel,' she said. She took down the album from the top of the bookshelf where it had been since Mammy had told me about Claudia. Once I had opened the album, I went straight to the picture of Claudia, the one where she was looking down at me in the crib. I put my index finger on the picture.

'Mammy told me this is my sister Claudia. Is that true?' I asked excitedly, looking at my mother.

The Green Elevator Cage

Except for the canary happily chirping in the background, there was absolutely no sound. The room had gone quiet.

Mum paused for a few seconds, took a deep breath, glanced furtively at her brother and mother, put her soft, warm hand on my forearm, kissed me on the forehead, and then calmly answered me.

'My darling Michel, Mammy is right. Claudia is your sister. She lives with her father in Switzerland. Her father and I were married in the Congo. But we didn't get along. That happens. So, we divorced. Claudia went with him, and you came with me,' she said. 'But you'll see her soon. I promise. She'd love to see you again.'

'When did I see her?'

'When you were two, when you came to live with Mammy and Uncle Pierre.'

I still couldn't believe I had a sister, but no one ever spoke about her, neither Mum, Mammy nor Uncle Pierre. Never. It was as if she didn't exist. I didn't understand.

'When will I see my father, Mum?'

'Soon, darling, soon.'

While thinking about Mum's answers, I turned the pages of the photo album, and there it was, a big picture of Mum wearing a long, beautiful white dress, pressed affectionately next to a very handsome, tall man, impeccably dressed in a white suit. I'll never forget that photograph. It took the whole page. They were a most beautiful couple straight out of a movie set of the '50s. So happy, so confident.

'Who's that man, Mum?'

'That's your father.'

'What's his name?'

19

'Hans, Hans Sigrist.'

I stared at the picture, touching it lightly, not quite understanding.

****

Except for the fact that my mother was more often than not away on trips, and I missed her dearly, I loved my little universe with Mammy and Uncle Pierre. There was a happy routine in which everyone had a part to play.

Mammy would always start the day by going to the calendar on the wall in the kitchen and marking a diagonal line, from top left to bottom right, in the square of that day and in the evening, before going to bed, a second diagonal line was marked across the square, leaving a very big X in the square. I remember thinking years later what a strange thing to do, as marking the days to countdown before her death, a liberation of sorts. After the calendar routine in the morning, she would remove the cloth covering our canary's cage and feed it. It would then sweetly chirp away, hopping about from one perch to the only other one.

Mammy would take me to my primary school which was just around the corner three or four blocks away. She would hold my hand and let it go only once I was in the courtyard and safely in the school. She would come back at lunch time to pick me up and bring me home so we could have our meal. And then we would head back to the school after lunch, where I would stay for two hours until she came once again to pick me up. We did this shuttle routine for two years. We knew it well. And everyone knew us in the neighbourhood. They knew how much my grandmother loved me and took good care of me. She always made sure that I was properly dressed. And, accordingly, people would comment on it on a regular basis.

'Bonjour Madame Van den Berghe. Isn't your little boy so well dressed as always,' they would say.

'Thank you very much,' she would answer each time, with lots of pride and satisfaction.

We would regularly go to the corner shop to get groceries, vegetables and fruit. The grocer would always give me a sweet or something he knew I liked. Going to the grocer's, the baker, or the butcher for that matter, was a social occasion. There was a lot of small talk, with questions about how my mother was going, when would she be back, and what grade is little Michel in now. But there was also a lot of waiting around. The grocer was very slow, and he was alone in managing the store. And regardless of how long it took to finally get served, you couldn't show your impatience.

I really liked going to the bakery, especially the one on Chaussée de Jette. We didn't go to that one that often because there was a bakery closer by. But when we did go, I was always looking forward to seeing the baker's daughter, who was so cute and charming. I think she was about two years older than me. Occasionally, Mammy would let me go alone to the bakery. That was always very exciting.

'Hello, Gretche,' I would say timidly.

'It's so nice to see you, Michel. What can I get you today?'

'12 rolls, please. My mother is visiting this week. I'm so excited.'

'You must be so happy. It must be difficult not to see your mother every day. I couldn't imagine not seeing mine all the time.'

I said nothing and simply looked down at the pastry, wondering how long Mum would be staying with us this time.

'Thanks, Gretche. See you next time.'

'See you next time, Michel,' smiling at me.

Many years later, when I was fourteen or so, I ran into her on the Belgian coast, somewhere close to Blankenberg. We were so pleased to have run into each other that we decided to spend some time alone in the dunes. The couple of intimate hours we spent exploring each other's bodies were so sweet, innocent and unforgettable. I will always remember that first opportunity to caress a girl's tender body, feel her softness, and smell her sweet, natural scent. I wonder sometimes whatever happened to sweet Gretche.

My other favourite stop in the weekly shopping was the butcher. I loved going there because he would always give me a slice of sausage or something like it. He never forgot. I liked him. He was fat and his white apron was always covered with blood stains from wiping his hands on it after each time he had handled the big slabs of raw meat. I liked the friendly atmosphere of the shop and the sawdust on the black and white chequered floor.

'And how are you today, Michel? Have you listened to your grandmother?' he would ask me each time.

And each time Mammy would respond, 'He's a real angel.'

I would smile.

'Well, that's great to hear, Madame Van den Berghe,' he would respond, as he gave me a cold-cut slice.

'Thank you very much, sir,' as I took the cold slice of charcuterie and took a big bite out of it.

Saturday morning was always a special day for me. This was the day Uncle Pierre would take me for a long walk to the city centre. Mammy would dress me up in my best going-out clothes. These usually consisted of grey shorts, black shoes, a white shirt, a bow tie and a jacket. I looked like an old man at the age of seven. Once ready, we would go off and start walking, for an hour or so. He would hold my hand the whole time as we meandered through the streets. Eventually, we would reach the 'Red light' district, which was on the way to the centre, so I was told by Uncle Pierre. I would always run off to the women in the windows.

'Look at the beautiful girls,' I would inevitably say each time I got to one of the windows where one or two of the ladies would be sitting on chairs dressed in clothes that left little to the imagination.

Uncle Pierre was in his mid-twenties. Like his father, Bonpa, he was in the army. And like his father, he was a sergeant. He was also a disciplinarian who believed homes should be run like army units, with no questions asked by the troops. But while he lived at home, Mammy was the boss, so there was no suggestion that he would be setting the law in the house, however much he tried. In any case, Uncle Pierre was always good to me, playing games with me whenever I asked him. I loved him dearly. He was to all intents and purposes my father.

When we would finally get to the city centre of Brussels, we would sit down at a sidewalk café and watch the people walk by. It was so much fun to comment on the dress code of the various passers-by. I would always have a Coke and Uncle Pierre would always have a beer. It was so pleasant to sit outside in the sun and enjoy the world going by. Women wore straight skirts and high heels and men wore slim suits and pointed shoes. Everyone was well dressed. Sadly, and most suddenly, this cosy little universe of mine came crashing down out of the blue.

****

One morning, I came into the kitchen, and I found my yellow canary at the bottom of the cage, on its back, its little legs straight up, rigid. Dead. This was my first encounter with death. I didn't know things died, that there was a finite time to everything. I was very sad. Still, my grandmother didn't buy another one. However, much worse was going to happen on that day.

Quite unexpectedly, at least for me, Mum came home, but not alone. She came with a tall man, with lots of blond hair and very tanned skin.

She bent down and hugged me so tenderly as she always did. She softly whispered into my ear, 'Hello my darling Michel.' I could smell her wonderful perfume enveloping me. 'This is John. We just got married. He's your new father. He's very excited to meet you.'

I was stunned. It was simply too much to take in for a seven-year-old boy who had only recently been told that he had a sister and had yet to meet his father. Mum hadn't told me that she was going to get married. Nothing. I didn't understand what this would mean but I did know that things wouldn't stay the same. And to make things worse, I didn't understand a word John said. He only spoke English. He was from a place called California. I had no clue where that was. Still, he seemed nice enough. He had brought me popcorn.

That afternoon was awkward and strange. And even though Mammy and Uncle Pierre seemed to like him, they too didn't understand anything he said. So, there was a lot of sign language and Mum did a lot of translating. But things would take a turn for the worse.

Someone came up with the idea that it might be a good get-to-know exercise if we played a game of Monopoly. I thought that was a great idea. I always won at Monopoly, so I very much looked forward to the game. I could show John how good I was. Unfortunately, things didn't pan out as expected. Very soon into the game, I could sense that it wasn't going my way at all. No one was landing on my properties, and I was landing on theirs. That had never happened before. So, the inevitable ensued. Not only did I lose, and lost badly at that, but I lost to this stranger from a place called California, who had invaded my safe world. He took all my hotels, all my houses and all my properties, and he chucked my pawn back in the box unceremoniously.

'Sorry, buddy boy but that's the way it goes.'

I was utterly shattered, my universe destroyed, having been humiliated by my new 'father'. I ran off to the back room and cried my eyes out. I couldn't stop crying. Mum eventually came to comfort me but also told me that I had to learn to lose.

'John thinks you are too big to be allowed to win each time. You're a big boy. And he has a point.'

Not only had I lost, but that day I learned that I wasn't as good at Monopoly as I thought I was. It had all been a sham. And my beautiful mother had sided with the stranger. Yes, my world had indeed changed forever, and there was much more to come down the line.

4

Brussels – Boarding School
(1969-1975)

'Don't forget to inhale deeply. The deeper, the better,' Martin said.

So, I deeply inhaled the Belga cigarette. The impact was immediate; my head spun, I felt very weak, and I couldn't think straight. I coughed like crazy. I honestly thought I was going to die. I regretted having decided to try smoking. We were outside at the back of my boarding school. It was around 7:30 pm, and it was dark and chilly. No one could see us, so there was no danger of getting caught by the headmaster. That was the beginning of my smoking experience. I was sixteen and I had already been in boarding school for three years. I'd be there for another three.

Martin was my closest friend. We met the first day I came to the Catholic boarding school, Collège Cardinal Mercier, in Waterloo, about thirty minutes south of Brussels. Mum had dropped me off on the first day a late afternoon in early September 1969. It was overcast and cold. I was thirteen years old. For the last five years, I had been living with Mum and John in Beirut, Lebanon, and in Jeddah, Saudi Arabia. In Beirut, I went to a French-speaking Jesuit-run school where teachers were nasty and brutal. In Jeddah, we lived in an American bubble which included going to an American school. Unfortunately, the Saudi authorities didn't allow the establishment of high schools for expatriate children. As a result, Mum and John decided I'd go to a French-speaking boarding school in Belgium. So, after living with Mum for only five years, going to boarding school thousands of kilometres away was the green elevator all over again. Daily parental hugs were now a memory.

My bedroom for the next six years would be a large room, with two rows of four single beds. Each boarder had a small built-in wardrobe. The washbasins, which only had cold water, were outside the room in a very long hallway. Seventy-two of them to be precise to accommodate nine teams, as each group of eight was called, of boys. After the lights were turned off the first night in the dormitory, tears quietly trickled down my cheeks. Desperately seeking comfort, I kissed the small silver St. Joseph pendant around my neck, which my grandmother had given me, whispering to myself, 'I miss you so much, Mum.' Silence and coldness hugged me for the rest of the night.

What I remember most of those boarding school days, particularly in the early years when I had few friends, was the sheer loneliness, day in, day out. The loneliness was like being alone in a rowboat in the middle of a deadly still ocean, with no land, nor ship in sight. Completely alone. Completely isolated. Most of the other boys probably endured the same feelings but the big difference with them was that my parents were thousands of kilometres away and theirs were somewhere in Belgium. And while the atmosphere of the boarding school was positive, and there was no hazing whatsoever, it was no substitute for the warmth of a parental home. And even though I'd see Mammy every weekend, she didn't understand what I was going through and I didn't tell her. She also couldn't help me with the educational side of things, having only gone to school up to grade three herself. I had to rely on myself. I had no choice.

The mail at boarding school always arrived after lunch. After we had finished eating our meal, all seventy-two of us would walk together on the five-minute stroll along the poplar-lined path from the cafeteria to the boarding house and we would walk through the large wooden doors at the entrance. As one walked into the foyer, one could see all the letters displayed on top of the closed lid of the upright black piano, like small windows into other worlds. I would easily spot from afar my mother's letter. She always used green ink, the envelopes were oblong with coloured stripes on the edges, and the letters were always adorned with exotic stamps. But what was most distinctive about her letters was the handwriting. It was one that I had never seen before and never would see elsewhere. The handwriting looked like stick characters dancing, frolicking, playing on the envelope waiting to be liberated so that they could perform for me, after having travelled so many thousands of kilometres to reach me. I would take the letter with me and settle somewhere quiet in the boarding school, usually on my bed, away from everyone else. I wanted to savour completely and slowly my Mum's words, ones that had been carefully, lovingly written on onion airmail paper from a faraway land, probably some three weeks earlier. The days I didn't get an expected letter were always very sad ones. I'll always remember Mum's first letter at boarding school. I cherished it, and I would read it over and over whenever I felt low and lonely. It would always lift my spirits.

Claude Rakisits

Jeddah, 23 September 1969

My dearest Michel,

By the time you read this letter, you will have been at the Collège for at least a month. I'm sure you are now all settled in, and you have made many friends. It's great that you can visit Mammy on the weekends and enjoy some of her food, especially her stewed rabbit which you like so much!

I was so sad to leave you at the boarding school. I cried so much on the train back to Brussels that people asked me in the train carriage if I was alright. I couldn't forget the sad expression in your eyes begging me to take you with me and away from the Collège. But as you know, we had no choice. Don't worry too much, Michel. This is one of the best schools in Belgium. And remember, education is everything.

The house feels very empty without you, especially when John is flying and staying overnight somewhere and I'm alone in the house. It's very strange to go by your room and not see you in there reading, studying or classifying your stamps. Anyway, it's ready for you when you'll come and visit at Christmas. The whole neighbourhood is actually very quiet because your friends have also had to leave to go to boarding school in the US or elsewhere.

It's very warm and humid here as you can well imagine. But, very oddly, it did rain hard almost non-stop for three days a few days ago. As a result, everything was flooded. Because there are no gutters, the souk was a total mess, with water rushing into the shops. Lots of shoppers' merchandise was simply floating away. The water was knee-high in some places. It was rather funny seeing all those men having to lift their white thobes. They looked very silly.

Other than that, everything is the same as when you left. Every morning Mohammed takes out the garbage and dumps it on the usual garbage heap on the corner of the street. You should have seen the street with all the rain. At one point I thought the car would get stuck and we'd have to get out of the car and step into the awful muddy mess. Anyway, all this mud hasn't stopped the usual animals from coming to the garbage heap for their breakfast. But yesterday, unusually, the camels came before the goats and buffaloes, followed by the wild dogs and cats. Even after all these years, I still can't get used to this filth and smell. At least in the Belgian Congo, the garbage was picked up!

We had a few people (Jane and Tom, Carol and Dick, Julie and Randy, and Susan and Burt) over last week for drinks (not that there is much choice for booze here, haha) and a bit of fun. We ended up having a great party. Even John danced! Dean Martin and Frank Sinatra songs were particularly popular with everyone.

Well, my darling Michel, I'm going to have to let you go so that I can give this letter to John so he can take it with him to the office and it can go off with the next mailbag to Europe.

We miss you so much. We are so proud of you. We know that you'll achieve great things later in life. Always believe in yourself.

Your loving mother. xxx

****

The good thing about going to boarding school in Belgium was that I finally got to meet Claudia. Now that we were on the same continent meant that we could visit each other more easily.

Our big reunion was at the time Mum dropped me off for the first time at boarding school. We had organised that Claudia would come to Brussels for a long weekend while Mum was still in Brussels before going back to Saudi Arabia. When the day arrived, I was nervous, anxious and excited all in one. I had been waiting so long for this moment. I was thirteen and Claudia was sixteen, and we hadn't seen each other since the Belgian Congo when we were both too young to remember. As for Mum, she'd only seen Claudia a couple of times since the divorce in 1957. Claudia's train, which was coming from Zurich, was arriving at 11:07 on Platform Six at Brussel's Gare du Nord train station. Claudia had sent me a small picture of herself a couple of weeks earlier so that I would know who to look for. She looked so pretty, with a little dimple on her chin. So cute.

The train arrived on time. Mum and I waited in anticipation as to where she'd get off from on the train. And then I saw her. It was like seeing an angel, a gift from the gods. She was so beautiful, with such a lovely smile. I ran towards her, and she hugged me so warmly. She wouldn't stop saying, 'Oh Michel, it's been so long, too

The Green Elevator Cage

long my dear little brother.' I was in tears, full of joy, happiness and sadness for all the years we'd missed out on. Mum was in tears as well, repeatedly saying to her, 'Oh my darling, I love you so much. I've missed you so much.' This was a moment I would never forget, ever. We couldn't touch each other enough. We were like birds preening each other.

We decided we'd go for lunch. We walked from the station to the restaurant. And even though it was a bit of a way, because we had so much to say to each other, we didn't mind the walk. Actually, it was a good way to get to know each other.

We found a restaurant in the Petite rue des Bouchers, very close to the Grand Place, in the centre of Brussels. It was a typical Belgian restaurant, where the waiters wore white aprons and spoke the local jargon. The tables all had white and red-chequered tablecloths. I decided to have my favourite dishes: cheese croquettes, followed by steak américain and french fries. We had so much to catch up on we didn't know where to start. We all spoke over each other, asking lots of questions in a desperate attempt to catch up with so much time lost. It was so much fun! We asked the waiter to take a picture of us with my little Kodak 104 camera I had brought for the occasion. As I handed the camera to the waiter, I thought of the small camera shop I had bought it from on Al Hamra Street in Beirut some four years earlier. And here we were taking a picture of the reunited family with it. But even with all the excitement, I really wanted to be alone with Claudia so we could have a serious conversation. I could sense she too wanted that. We decided to take a taxi home to Mammy's apartment on Boulevard Leopold II.

We were all excited as we piled into the little green cage to make the trip up to the fourth floor. This time the trip was a happy one; I was with Mum and Claudia. I wasn't being left behind begging for Mum to stay. I was coming home with her and my sister. Claudia was very nervous. She held my hand and squeezed it tightly as the cage went up. I couldn't wait for her to meet Mammy whom she had never met. I looked up to Claudia and she smiled at me, nervous, anxious, not knowing what to expect. Mum was all animated, completely oblivious to what Claudia was going through.

We finally arrived in silence after what felt like an eternity. Mammy was waiting for us on the landing, with a great welcoming smile. First Mum came out and gave Mammy a big hug. I then came out and hugged Mammy the way I always did. And then Claudia came out. There was just the merest hint of an awkward moment, which we all felt, during which no one knew how things would go from here on. But Mammy opened her arms wide, her eyes tearing up, with her voice slightly trembling, and said, 'You are such a beautiful young woman Claudia, so beautiful. Come in my arms my dearest.' She hugged Claudia and held her tightly in her arms, kissing the side of her head many times. 'I'm so, so happy to finally see you after all those years. It's been too long.' I could see Claudia smiling contently.

Mum and I were in tears. We were finally all together again as a family in the same place where I had first found out about Claudia so many years earlier. I was so happy. The three most important women in my life were here with me. Life was good.

That evening, Claudia and I finally had time to ourselves. Time to talk to each other. Time to find out who we were. We were strangers and we needed to discover each other quickly because we had so little time to spare but so much to cover. We were sitting in the living room. We were both sitting cross-legged on the brown couch. We were all smiles, full of happiness. Mum and Mammy had gone to bed. There were two side lights on. Nothing else.

'I can't believe that this is actually happening after all those years,' I said with a big smile across my face.

'Me too. I've been waiting for this moment for years. Dreaming how it would be. Would we get along? What you looked like? Would you be funny? I'm so happy to finally see you again since the Congo.'

'But we did write to each other, like pen pals,' I said.

She smiled. 'Yes, we did. That was great. And I got great stamps from you from Saudi Arabia and Lebanon.'

'Claudia, I've been wanting to ask this for years. I can't wait any longer. But why is it that our father hasn't been in touch with me?'

There was a long pause. She looked down and gently caressed the green cushion she had been holding the whole time. 'I've asked him that as well, several times but each time he won't answer me. I'm sorry to say this to you Michel, but it's as if you don't exist. He has made it very clear that he doesn't want to talk about you. I tell him that I have a right to see my brother. He just tells me that if I want to see you, I can go to Brussels.'

'I don't understand Claudia. I often think about it, thinking why he wouldn't want to see his son.'

'I know. It must be very hurtful for you.'

'It is. I don't know what to think. I really don't. But I think we should talk to Mum tomorrow morning and see what she thinks about it all. Maybe she'd be able to talk to him and get him to change his mind.'

'That's a good idea, Michel.'

'You know, Claudia, I have this photograph of you and me in the Congo. I hold onto it for dear life because it's the only one I have of the two of us together. Look, I'll show you. Don't move.'

I went to the large bookcase in the dining room and on the bottom shelf, there was a small tin box, the size of a shoe box. The cover of it had a picture of King Baudouin and Queen Fabiola. I brought the box back with me and I sat next to Claudia on the couch. I was so excited to share this picture with my dear sister. I had been waiting for this moment for so very long. I couldn't believe this was actually happening. I slowly lifted the lid to the tin box. And there on the very top was an old faded, black and white picture of a three-year-old girl wearing a cute little, white dress, looking down lovingly at a baby in a large white crib. You could see the legs of small African children in the background.

'Oh, that's incredible, Michel, I've never seen this picture,' she said, in total amazement.

'It's the photograph that I first saw when I was six and which revealed that I had a sister. Until then no one had told me that you existed. No one. I was so shocked I hadn't been told. But I was also so excited to meet you and find out who you were.'

She delicately took the picture out of the box and looked at it intensely.

'You really don't have one, or one like it?'

'No, I have nothing of us together.'

'I have often looked at it, wondering what it would have been had we never been separated so many years ago. If we'd always been together either here in Belgium or in Switzerland.'

After Claudia had completely absorbed the meaning of the photo, she gave it back to me and I returned it to its home in the tin box which contained other pictures and letters from Mum. This was my treasure box, my dearest possession.

'Let's check the photo albums tomorrow to see if we can find photographs you can take back with you.'

'Great idea!'

We spent the rest of the evening talking about so many things, like the universe, friends, Saudi Arabia, Lebanon, Claudia's half-siblings, her stepmother, Mum, John, stamps, and everything else in between.

'You know it's in this room where I lost for the first time a game of Monopoly, and it was John who beat me on the first day I met him. I'll never forget it. I was so crushed and devastated.'

'That would have been so awful for you.'

'It's a long time ago, but still, it was a strange way to get to meet one's stepfather.'

'How do you get along with him?'

'Fine. He treats me very well. He doesn't hit me like so many fathers do, especially American fathers. But I'm not really close to him. He's a bit strange and he can be very moody for no real reason. But he loves and respects Mum a lot. That's important.'

The next morning, after breakfast, Claudia and I were sitting with Mum in the living room. Mammy had gone to church. Claudia and Mum were sitting on the brown sofa, and I was sitting in an armchair across from them. I was nervous, but I took a deep breath, and I asked Mum the question.

'Mum, Claudia and I wanted to ask you something that's been bothering us for a long time.'

'Yes, darling, what is it?' She looked nervous.

'Why is it that our father has never been in touch with me? Why? Doesn't he care about me?'

Silence.

Looking at me, almost staring, she said, 'I don't know Michel, I really don't know. I don't know what to say.' And, then turning to Claudia and putting her hand on Claudia's leg, she said, 'You know Hans can be very stubborn and intransigent. I'll get in touch with him and see what I can do, but I can't promise anything.'

'Thank you, Mum. Thank you so much,' I said as I got up to get some more coffee. I hugged her and gave her a big kiss. Claudia looked at me and smiled with her eyes.

5

Brussels – The Wake (2000)

Max didn't recognise Mammy, as she lay there in an open coffin at the funeral parlour close to the retirement home, where she had been living for the last five years. Her soul had vanished, only an empty, meaningless shell remained. It could have been any old woman he was looking at. He wanted to remember her as the warm, loving grandmother, instead, he was standing in front of a cold cadaver in a shockingly uninviting room. He didn't cry. He left the room after five minutes.

Waiting in the adjoining room were his mother, Claudia, Uncle Pierre and his wife, Jeannette. Max thought that this wake was turning a bit into a long-overdue family reunion. Max hadn't seen his mother since 1990 when he visited her briefly in Florida on his way to an academic conference in Washington. And as for his sister and Uncle Pierre, except for a couple of short trips to Europe, he had hardly seen them in 20 years, when he left Belgium to go to Canada in 1976. Claudia looked charming and lovely as always, with her cutest little chin dimple. Uncle Pierre looked very fit for someone in his late 50s. He had lots of thick black hair, just as he remembered him from before. But Max also knew that Uncle Pierre was vain and that he undoubtedly dyed his hair. Jeannette, whom Uncle Pierre had married some ten years earlier after his first wife was killed in a horrible car accident, seemed pleasant enough, having never met her.

All five were standing uncomfortably in silence in the room not really knowing what to do next. But Uncle Pierre quickly took control of the situation as if he was still in the army which he had left 20 years earlier.

'Now that we've all spent a few last moments with Mammy, the undertakers will set everything up in the main hall, including bringing in the coffin. The others are already there waiting. There are seats reserved for us at the very front. After the ceremony, which will not take long, we're going to go to the restaurant, Le Royal, which I booked.' Looking around, he asked, 'Everyone okay with that?'

Silence.

Max nodded, as did his mother.

Turning to Max's mum, 'Juliette, why don't you lead the way into the hall?' Uncle Pierre suggested, without giving her any option to refuse.

She was wearing a small black, woman's hat with a laced veil which she had brought down over her face. Uncle Pierre had insisted she wore such attire out of respect for their mother and the rest of the family. Again, she had been given no option.

There must have been some fifteen people or so already seated in the cold, cavernous hall, in three rows of seats. Max hadn't seen them in at least twenty years, if not more. Many he didn't recognise. Quite a number were relatives of Mammy's, old sisters and even older brothers and some of their adult children. He vaguely remembered seeing them when he'd visited them in Mammy's village when he was only a small boy. That was his Flemish tribe, he thought. He discreetly waved at some of them and nodded at others. It was all a bit awkward.

The coffin was already there. Alone. Waiting. Silent. Observing.

Piped through the sound system, they played Schubert's Ave Maria sung by Pavarotti. Uncle Pierre had asked Max to choose a piece which he thought Mammy would have liked. As soon as Pavarotti began to sing, Max knew he wouldn't be able to hold back the tears. It was too hard. It all came flooding back, all jumbled up, the days walking together to the shops, to the butcher, to school, in the park, with Mammy holding his hand, having breakfast together in the kitchen, the sweet yellow canary. His visits to his grandfather's tomb, his medals. He held onto his mother's hand. They played another four pieces, including Chopin's Nocturne C sharp minor and Beethoven's Piano Sonata No. 14 in C-sharp minor. When the music stopped, everyone rose and walked out quietly. Most people were discreetly wiping their eyes. People mingled outside waiting for the taxis to arrive, while others walked away to their cars.

The lunch went well, at least for most of the time. The restaurant was a traditional Belgian establishment, with white and red chequered tablecloths. Pictures of the King and Queen of the Belgians and other royal members were hung everywhere, as were pictures of various public events at which royal members were prominent. They had put tables together to form two long rows, allowing for the twenty guests to comfortably sit around the tables.

There was no special seating arrangement, but it was clear that Uncle Pierre and Juliette would sit at the centre of one of the rows, across from each other. Max sat to his mother's right and Claudia sat next to him. Jeannette sat next to Pierre, across from Max. Everyone else fell into place. Bottles of red wine were already waiting on the tables; the white wine came as soon as everyone was sitting. Once the wine started to flow, the conversation became more relaxed. This was a time to catch up on lost time and gossip.

'So, Max, how's Australia treating you?' Uncle Pierre asked in his usual bellowing, authoritative voice. 'Happy there?'

'Yes, very happy. It hasn't always been plain sailing but now things are really good. I can't believe I've already been there eighteen years. Anyway, it's probably the best decision I've ever made,' Max said, as he sipped his white wine. 'But I know Mum wouldn't completely agree with that, would you?' Max added, glancing at his mother and tapping gently on her forearm.

'You are right, darling. I'm not crazy about having you so far away but as long as you visit once in a while that's fine.'

'Of course, Mum,' Max said, thinking about how lonely his wedding had been with no family members in attendance.

'Anyway, I'm really pleased we could all make it to Mammy's funeral,' said Uncle Pierre. 'And I'm particularly happy that you could make it all the way from Australia, Max, because I know how much Mammy meant to you and how important she had been for you in the early years of your life.'

'Absolutely. It's wonderful that you could make it, Max,' Juliette said, touching her son's arm.

'I wouldn't have missed it for anything. Absolutely not,' Max said. 'I'm sorry that Jane and Genevieve couldn't make it, but I'm sure you understand why.'

'Of course, we do son,' Uncle Pierre said. Hearing Pierre's comforting words reminded Max of how his uncle had been such an important part of his early life.

Max had pushed his chair back a bit so that Claudia on his right could feel part of the conversation.

'Just in case you were to ask me, I've brought a few pics with me of my two favourite girls.' Max pulled out a bunch of pictures from inside his tweed jacket. He passed them around, briefly commenting on each one. It was an easy way to bring other people sitting around the table to join in. More wine was poured, and more bottles of wine were brought to the tables. By the time the food arrived most guests had already had plenty of wine, and no one seemed to care about the quality of the food, or what was actually being served.

After the dessert, as people began to mingle and swap seats so that they could meet up with other family members and friends, Max turned to Claudia.

'I'm sorry I haven't chatted with you more, but there are so many people to catch up with.'

'Don't worry, Max. It's interesting for me to meet unknown members of my tribe, as you like to say.'

'I know what you mean. I've really been detribalised because I really don't have much in common with any of them. So don't feel too lonely,' Max said with his usual grin.

Claudia picked up her glass of wine and they clinked their glasses. 'Prost,' she said.

'A notre santé,' Max responded. 'I'm so happy you came, Claudia. I know you don't know many of these people. But Mum is really happy you came. And anyway, it's great to be able to catch up. It's been so long since we last saw each other. I often think of our fantastic trip to Lubumbashi in the DC-4. Do you realise it's been twenty-four years since that trip?'

'That trip is one of the highlights of my life. I'll always treasure it. I still have the small, black wooden elephant John got me from that little African boy.'

'Well, speaking of gifts, of course, I still have the beautiful silver lighter you gave me on the plane.'

'Oh yes, I had forgotten about it.'

'But because I stopped smoking many years ago, I no longer use it.'

'Well, that's very good news.'

'You're right. But I've put it in a safe place with all the things I value a lot.'

They each took a sip of their wine.

'You're right, it's been way too long since we last met. But you're the one who decided to go and live in Australia. It's not what I call next door.'

'I know what you mean. But we all have our lives to live, our happiness to find.' He poured himself some more white wine and topped up Claudia's glass.

They sat in silence for a few moments.

'How are you going otherwise? Happy? How's the painting going?'

'I'm well and I'm happy. My painting is doing fine. I paint quite a bit, but I don't sell as much as I would like. That's probably the case for all painters.'

'Remember that Van Gogh sold nothing while alive.'

'I know, but I'm not sure if that's good news or that I have to wait till I die to become famous.'

Max took a sip of his wine and played around with the breadcrumbs on the table.

'I suppose in a way I am a bit like Van Gogh because without Jürgen supporting me, I'd be starving,' Claudia said.

'How's Jürgen going?'

'He's doing well. His architectural firm is doing very well and he's happy with the team working for him.'

'I know I haven't seen much of him over the last 15 years, but I like him. Please pass on my warmest regards.'

'I will, thank you.'

Glancing around the room, Max said, 'I'd better talk to a few other people I haven't seen in many, many years. But we'll have plenty of time to catch up tomorrow as well.'

'Of course, not a problem. I'll talk to Mum a bit,' she said, patting his forearm with her hand. 'I'm so happy to see you after all this time.'

'Me too.' They hugged each other.

Max got up and looked around. Most people seemed to have moved from their original assigned seats, with the many simultaneous conversations generating a congenial atmosphere. The wine was flowing liberally. Max thought how ironic it was that it often took a death in the family to bring people together. He spotted his cousin, Chantal, his late Aunt Sylvie's daughter, whom he hadn't seen for a very long time, but with whom he used to go partying a lot before leaving for Canada. He chatted with her and her husband, Patrick, for a while. He used to be a very successful gunrunner in the Congo, but he had hit hard times recently, with the Russians muscling into this lucrative market. He was now playing the stock market with money he didn't have. That wasn't going so well. But he still behaved as if he had a million dollars in the bank. He was a charming individual who sailed very close to the wind of legality.

Patrick and Uncle Pierre hated each other. No one could remember how their intense dislike of each other had started but it was now an integral part of the family equation. After promising Chantal and Patrick they'd catch up for lunch before going back to Australia, Max went to speak to Chantal's brother, Robert, who was only a couple of years older than him. He had gone to the seminary but after four years of committing to God, he fell in love with Jean, another seminarian, and decided to commit to him instead. They both gave up the religious path and now ran a successful counselling service for teenagers at a loss with life. It wasn't clear what role God played in their lives, but Max suspected this was no ménage à trois. After wishing them well, he bid them goodbye and decided to have a chat with Uncle Pierre and his wife Jeannette.

'Sorry I haven't had more of a chat with you guys yet, but I've had a lot of catching up to do with all the relatives I haven't seen in many years,' Max said, as he pulled over a chair to get closer to them.

'Not to worry, son,' Uncle Pierre said.

'I'm happy I can finally meet you after all those years,' Max said, as he turned to Jeannette.

'Pierre has often spoken about you, especially about your earlier years when you all lived with Mammy,' Jeannette said.

'Yes, Uncle Pierre thought I was one of his soldiers, forcing me on long walks in Brussels on weekends. He drilled into me the benefits of walking. And actually, I now love walking. Thank you, Uncle!' Max said as he raised his wine glass to them.

'We'll drink to that,' Uncle Pierre said. 'You know, darling, I've known this kid since he was only about this high,' putting his hand out only about one metre off the ground. 'He's like a son to me.'

'You were very good to me. I will never forget it.'

'I effectively raised you. Don't you forget that.'

'I won't, trust me. You'll make sure I don't,' Max said, with a cheeky grin. 'So how long have you been in retirement?'

'Coming to three years in a couple of months.'

'Are you enjoying living on the coast?'

'Yes, it's very relaxing; better than being in Washington,' Uncle Pierre said.

'It sounds like you didn't like living in the US?' Max said.

'It's a beautiful country, but the politicians are mostly idiots, and people act like cowboys with their guns everywhere.'

'I know what you mean but that's not really a reason to dismiss a whole country.'

'For a superpower and the leader of the so-called Free World, most Americans are totally ignorant of the outside world,' Jeannette said.

'I think we need to drink something stronger than this wine if we are going to have this discussion,' Uncle Pierre said. 'I'm going to order a 'half and half'. You want one?'

'What's in it?' Max asked.

'Half cognac, half Cointreau.'

'Sounds pretty lethal!'

'You can handle it.' Uncle Pierre went off to the bar.

Max and Jeannette made small talk about nothing and how well the lunch had gone.

Uncle Pierre came back with two small glasses filled with what looked like petrol. 'Here, take one. It's good for you,' he said, as he gave him one of the glasses.

Max took a sip. 'Wow, this is pretty strong stuff.'

'It's meant to be. It puts hair on your chest.'

'It also scrapes your insides.'

'So how long are you in Brussels for?' Jeannette asked.

'Only for three more days, and then I go back.'

'Coming back to what we were talking about before, I don't understand how Juliette can live in the US for good,' Uncle Pierre said.

'Maybe it has something to do with the fact that John is American.'

'Sure. It doesn't give her much choice.'

'But tell me, why is it that ever since I can remember you've always been so negative about Americans? They did, after all, liberate Europe from the nasty Germans. As you know, the Europeans wouldn't have been capable of doing so without their help!' Max knew he had hit a raw nerve, but he was tired of hearing all those same anti-American sentiments.

'You've been brainwashed son,' Uncle Pierre said, as he swallowed the last of his toxic mix. 'I'm getting another two more of these. I think we need it.' Before Max could say anything, Uncle Pierre was off to the bar.

There was more useless, fill-in-the-time, small talk between Max and Jeannette about the weather in Belgium compared to the weather in America.

After handing over another glass of 'half and half' to Max, Uncle Pierre sat down heavily on his chair, visibly upset and unhappy.

'Do you really think the Yanks came to liberate us because they loved us? Uncle Pierre asked rhetorically, taking a sip from his toxic brew. 'They came because it was in their interest.'

'So what? They still lost thousands of young men in the process. And they got you out from under the Nazi boot,' Max said, taking a sip from his drink. 'The problem is that the European ego was chipped by having to rely on raw, unsophisticated American power to save itself.'

'That's utter crap what you are saying.'

'I don't think so. It's the predictable behaviour of someone who hates the one who rescued them. The dependency syndrome.'

'Don't use your academic shit with me,' Uncle Pierre said.

'I'm not. I'm just stating the bleeding obvious.' Max knew that he was winning the argument because Uncle Pierre was starting to play the man and not the ball. He took a sip of his glass.

'And let's be frank, you never liked John because he's American and he effectively took me away from you.'

Silence.

'I can tell you one thing for certain, I'll never return to the US, even for your mother's funeral.'

Silence.

'Boys, maybe we should move on and talk about something else?' Jeannette said, trying desperately to lighten the situation.

'That's really, really nasty what you just said. I can't believe you would think that, let alone say it, especially at your mother's wake,' Max said, finishing with one gulp what was left in his glass.

'Well, I see you guys are in deep discussion. What are you guys talking about that's got you so worked up?' Juliette asked, having just come back with Claudia.

'Nothing, Mum. Just talking politics. A couple of different viewpoints,' Max said, lightly.

'Right… anyway, I was thinking of going to the hotel with Claudia and having an early night. Do you want to come with us, Max?'

'Sounds like a good idea. I've had plenty to drink.'

'Pierre, I was planning on going to Mammy's room with Claudia and Max tomorrow morning and have a look at the stuff that she's left behind. We could meet here for lunch tomorrow, let's say at 12:30, so we can discuss how we might want to divide up some of the more sentimental items. What do you think?' Juliette asked.

'Yeah, sure. That's fine,' Uncle Pierre said, slightly slurring his words.

'Okay, we'd better go. Thank you, Pierre, for organising this lunch. I think it went very well.'

'Not a problem. I think it did go well.' Uncle Pierre got up and everyone gave each other the customary cheeky kisses.

Uncle Pierre and Max shook hands. 'You've changed, really changed,' he said to Max.

Max ignored the comment.

The Green Elevator Cage

As they waited outside for a taxi, Juliette asked Max what Pierre's comment was all about.

'Nothing Mum, just Uncle Pierre being silly and having had too much to drink.'

Max thought that funerals were in many ways like weddings; they brought out the best and the worst of people.

****

Juliette, Claudia and Max went into Mammy's room at the retirement home early the next morning. In the middle of the room, the assistants had placed a green metal trunk, like the one Max had used to come to Australia. It was the standard Belgian Congo-issued travelling kit. Like the coffin the day before, it was waiting there alone, quiet and listening. But the difference was that in this case, it was waiting to be opened. It wanted to be opened. The room smelled of death, or rather the smell of disinfectant to cover the smell of death. As Max looked around the room, at the worn-away armchair, the empty bed, the blackness of the television, the fading pictures of family members, some of them having already long gone, he thought of Jacques Brel's ever so poignant song, "Les Vieux". In his song, old peoples' universe is reduced to movements from the bed to the armchair and then to the window, then simply from the bed to the armchair, and finally simply to the bed, never to leave again. He could feel his eyes tearing up.

'Mum, I need to go out for a few minutes. I won't be long.'

'Of course, darling, take your time.'

The trunk, which was three-quarters full of a mixed bag of items of all sizes and ages, was a real treasure trove; books on the Belgian Congo, pictures, some framed, some not, paraphernalia of souvenirs picked up and gifted over the years, letters from Juliette from exotic places and faraway lands, several African masks and wooden sculptures, notebooks and photo albums. Bonpa's picture in his military uniform and all his medals next to him like fallen soldiers buried with their leader were the first things they saw as they opened the trunk. Max had come to know those medals so well as a child as he went to sleep every night.

Juliette bent over and picked up the framed picture of her father as if for the first time.

'He was only fifty-one years old when he died. So young. You have so many of his ways, Max. And like you, he wasn't flexible,' Juliette said, as she looked at the picture in her hands. She kissed it and then put the picture down on the empty bed. She then picked up the frame with the medals. 'All those decorations. What good did it do him at the end?' She asked aloud, her voice quivering slightly, as she put it down next to the picture. 'Pierre will want those medals, but I want them so that you can have them, Max.'

'He'll put up a fight on this, Mum. You know that, right?'

'Yes, I do. But I still want them. Let's see how we go tomorrow.'

For the next two and half hours, the three of them went through the trunk, together and separately, rediscovering objects and memories long forgotten and unveiling secrets which had been hidden from most.

They found a photo album which Mammy had haphazardly put together in no special chronological order.

'Let's have a look at this together,' Juliette said, as she sat down in the armchair and Claudia and Max sat on either side of her on the wide wings of the armchair.

One of the first pictures they saw was the black and white photograph of three-year-old Claudia looking at Michel sleeping in a white crib resting on the ground. The picture had revealed by accident almost forty years earlier that Michel had a sister. At the bottom of the picture Juliette had written, "Lagos May 1956".

'I didn't know we lived in Lagos, Mum!' Claudia said, surprised by the discovery.

'Neither did I,' Max said.

'We were there for about three months because from what I can remember Hans's company needed him to go there to finalise a big engineering project.'

'Are there any other surprises we haven't heard of Mum?' Max asked.

'No, I don't think so. After Lagos, we went back to Leopoldville, where we stayed until I left for Belgium with you when you were about one year old, and Claudia went to Zurich with Hans.'

'How did you feel about all that Mum?' Claudia asked.

'I was so, so sad, so painful darling,' Juliette said, holding Claudia's hand. 'No mother should ever be separated from her child, but I had done wrong, and I was paying the price for it.'

'Oh Mum, you were so young,' Max said, as he put his arm around her shoulder.

'I was, but poor Claudia paid the price for my mistake.' Juliette began to weep quietly. 'I can only imagine the unhappiness I caused you, darling.' She wiped her tears with a handkerchief she took out of the light jacket she was wearing. 'I'm so sorry, darling.'

'I was sad, yes, very sad sometimes, but that's all a long time ago Mum. We must forget all that,' Claudia said, as she kissed the top of her mum's head.

'Thank you, Claudia. You know I love you so much.'

'I know you do. I love you too. Now let's look at other pictures.'

The next black and white picture they saw, as they turned the page, was one of Michel, who would have been about six, wearing his Sunday best, with his mother wearing a colourful floral dress. They are standing outside 209 Boulevard Leopold II, presumably about to go on a walk to the park.

'I look like an old man at the age of six,' Max said.

'No, you don't. You were very cute,' Juliette said.

A couple of pages further along, there was a picture of Juliette with Claudia in the snow. She would have been about seven, wearing skiing gear and looking happy to be with Mum.

'Look how fat I was when I was a child,' Claudia said.

'Not at all. That was just baby fat. Also, the puff jacket makes it look worse.'

'Mum, why didn't you come and visit me more often in Switzerland?' Claudia asked.

Silence.

'Your dad didn't make it easy for me to visit. And then I was travelling a lot. But you know I would have come more often if I could have,' she said.

'I know Mum. It's just that I was very sad not to see you more often.'

'I'm so sorry darling,' Juliette said, as she squeezed Claudia's hand. 'But look, we're together now, and that's important.'

'Yes, of course.'

Juliette resumed turning the pages.

'Oh look, the two of you with John in Lubumbashi sitting at a restaurant for lunch.'

'That was such a great trip,' Max said. 'You really should have come with us. You would've loved it, and it would have been really nice to have you with us.'

'I know. Anyway, that's the way it is,' quickly turning the page.

A few pages further, there was a picture of Max with Sophie. Max remembered that day well. They had put the camera on a timer so they could both be in front of the 21 long-stemmed red roses he had bought for her birthday.

'What is Sophie up to these days?' Juliette asked.

'She got married for a second time and has two kids, a boy and a girl.'

'So, you're still in touch?'

'Yes, but really through birthday cards and at Christmas only.'

'You were so in love with her, Max.'

'I was. But it's good it all ended otherwise there would have been no Jane and no Genevieve. Anyway, let's move on.'

The next picture they focussed on was one of Max in Balochistan during his field trip to Pakistan in 1983. He was wearing an Afghan pancake hat and was standing outside the run-down hotel he was staying at in Quetta.

'Thank you for sending me postcards, Max, I really enjoyed following you around Pakistan,' Claudia said.

'I was really worried for you when you were out there,' Juliette said. 'It's not as if Pakistan is the safest place in the world.'

'I know. But it always looks worse from the outside. I actually never felt in danger. It was such a great experience.'

And then the album abruptly stopped, Mammy having obviously decided to stop filling it.

They went back to the trunk to continue foraging through it. They unearthed three framed pictures. One was of the three of them at the restaurant where they had lunch when they all finally met for the first time. Max was thirteen and Claudia was sixteen. It was a day Max would never forget.

'I was so happy that day, Mum, to finally meet my little brother,' Claudia said, smiling warmly at Max.

'It was a great day for everyone,' Juliette said, 'really great.'

'Do you think I could have this picture, Mum?' Claudia asked.

'Of course, you can darling. You don't mind do you, Max?' Juliette said, turning to Max.

'Not at all. Anyway, we have other similar ones somewhere else.'

'Thank you so much. I'll give it a special place in my home.'

The other picture was also of the three of them with Mammy and Uncle Pierre on the Belgian coast in the summer of 1971, almost forty years earlier.

'No one seems to have changed at all since,' Max said with a smile on his face.

'No, not at all,' Juliette responded with good humour. Everyone giggled.

The third framed picture was of Max's wedding in 1992. It was a group photo of the whole wedding party. Being surrounded by several members of Jane's family made the absence of any member of Max's family that much starker.

'I'm sorry no one came to your wedding Max. But we would have if we could have done so,' Juliette said.

'Sure... Don't worry about it. Let's forget about it,' Max said flatly, as he went back to rummaging through the trunk.

He found a smallish red box with jewellery in it, including Mammy's wedding ring and the special ring that Mammy never took off.

'Look what I found Mum,' showing her the rings.

Picking up the special gold ring, Mum said, 'This ring Bonpa bought for Mammy just before our departure for the Belgian Congo in 1947. It's pink gold with their initials intertwined on the top. You can't see it anymore because it's all worn out. She loved it so much, she never took it off, ever. Here try it on your pinkie.' Max tried it on, and it fit perfectly on his right hand.

'It looks really good on your hand. I think you should get it because it would mean a lot to you. You don't mind, do you, Claudia?'

'Not at all. And he did live with Mammy for so many years. And I believe she would have wanted it that way,' Claudia said.

'Thank you so much. This means so much to me. Like Mammy, I will never take it off. It'll connect me to her and the Congo forever.'

'We'll just have to make sure Pierre is okay with that too,' said Juliette.

They went back to the trunk.

They found a small metal 8mm film canister with a film in it. On the lid in Juliette's distinctive handwriting is written, "Swimming pool with Hans, Juliette, Michel, Suzanna, Claudia and baby Michel, Leopoldville, November 1956."

'Do you remember what's on this movie, Mum?' Max asked.

'Darling, how would I remember? It's over forty years old.'

'We must watch it! We just need to bring it to a photography shop to have it turned into a VHS tape which we can then watch together. I can do that this afternoon after lunch. We can easily rent a VCR for a couple of hours,' Max said.

'That's a great idea, Max! I'd love to see it too,' Claudia said.

'Okay, if you can organise it that would be great,' Juliette said.

****

'So, how did you go with Mammy's stuff?' Uncle Pierre asked after they had all settled down and ordered the food and drinks. He was sitting at one end of a small table, with Juliette to his right and Jeannette to his left. Max sat next to his mum and Claudia was across from him, next to Jeannette.

'It went well. We discovered a lot of stuff we hadn't seen in years, if ever,' Juliette said.

'I know. She did keep things to herself,' Uncle Pierre said.

'After going through the whole trunk, there are only two things we're really interested in,' Juliette said. 'The other thing that makes things easier is that I spoke to Chantal and Robert yesterday, and they aren't interested in anything that belonged to Mammy.'

'Well, that will indeed make things easier,' Uncle Pierre said. 'Well, what are the two things you'd like?' He took a sip of his red wine.

'I'd like Max to have Mammy's special Congo ring Bonpa gave her in 1946. It'd mean a lot to him, and to me as well actually,' Juliette said.

'I don't see any problem with that. I think Mammy would have been very happy with him wearing it.'

'Thank you. I really appreciate it,' Max said.

'I still love you, son, even though you said silly things yesterday,' Uncle Pierre said, patting Max's forearm.

'We both did.'

Uncle Pierre took a sip of his wine. 'What's the other thing you're interested in.'

'I'd like Bonpa's medals,' Juliette said.

'Why?' Pierre said, surprised. 'You don't even know what each medal is and why he was awarded them.'

'So? What difference does that make?'

'As an ex-military man, I would appreciate them more.'

'That's ridiculous what you're saying. I don't need to have been in the army for thirty years to know that he deserved each of these medals.'

'Anyway, why are you interested in them all of a sudden?'

'What do you mean I'm suddenly interested in them?'

'Exactly that. You didn't even seem to be too interested in him when he was alive.'

'And what's that meant to mean?' Juliette asked, her voice breaking slightly.

'Where were you when he was dying in the hospital? You were frolicking around in Brussels with all your male entourage.'

'What?!'

'You know exactly what I'm referring to.'

'What would you know what I was doing? You were a fifteen-year-old kid.'

'You were so busy going to parties, you didn't know what time of the day it was. You'd come home early in the morning, just before Mammy got up. I could hear you.'

'I don't need a lecture from you.'

'You don't even know who's Max's father.'

'What did you just say?!' Juliette said, dumbstruck by the accusation.

'You heard me the first time,' taking a long sip of his wine.

Long silence.

'You need to apologise to Mum for what you've just said,' Max said to Uncle Pierre, his voice slightly shaky, having never spoken to his uncle in that tone.

'Really? I don't think so. I'm just stating the obvious fact,' as he poured more wine into his glass.

Silence.

'Do you actually know who's your biological father?'

'As a matter of fact, I do,' Max said, with total confidence in his voice. 'But the bottom line is that it's absolutely none of your fucking business,' spewing the words with utter bitterness.

'Now that you've made abundantly clear what you think of my personal life, can we come back to the medals?' Juliette said.

'It's very simple. The only things I want from Mammy's things are the medals. You can have everything else. I don't care,' Uncle Pierre said.

Silence.

'In any case, as the only son and a military man, Bonpa would have wanted me to have them.'

'Are you seriously going to use a male chauvinist argument to try to convince me that you have a greater claim to them than me?'

'Call it whatever you want, but I know that's what he would have wanted.'

'Oh, I see. So, you've been talking to him beyond the grave now?' With sarcasm dripping off her lips, she took a sip of her wine.

Silence. Jeannette and Claudia, effectively bystanders, were very uncomfortable, not knowing what to do or where to look.

'I can just as legitimately argue that as the oldest living child, I have a greater right to them than you do.'

Silence.

'Sorry to cut into your conversation, but you're obviously not going anywhere with this discussion,' Jeannette said, having listened quietly to the whole argument from the beginning. 'Maybe you guys should sleep on it and come back to it tomorrow.'

'Thank you for trying to fix things, Jeannette. I appreciate it. But you know, after what Pierre said, and his really hurtful and nasty comments, he can keep Bonpa's medals,' Juliette said.

'Oh, Juliette, don't take it like that,' Uncle Pierre said, reaching out to Juliette's hand, which she quickly pulled away.

'Don't give me this fake sweet voice now. You showed your true feelings towards me and what you think of my life. I don't think there's anything more to talk about today. I'm going back to the hotel.' Juliette rose. 'Max, could I ask you to make sure we cover our share of the lunch?'

'Of course, Mum. Leave it with me. You want me to come with you?' Max asked.

'Not it's okay. I'll be fine.'

Max got up and gave his mother a big hug and kiss. 'I love you, Mum,' he said.

'I love you too, darling.'

'I'll come with you Mum,' Claudia said. Max kissed Claudia goodbye.

Juliette and Claudia then left the restaurant.

'I'm going to get myself a scotch at the bar,' Max said, leaving Uncle Pierre and Jeannette at the table.

When Max came back to the table they were still there. He sat down heavily.

'So, what was all that about the way you spoke to Mum? It was nasty and completely uncalled for. And all this at Mammy's wake.'

Silence.

'Clearly, there must be something else that must be bothering you.' Max took a sip from his scotch. Uncle Pierre took a gulp of his red wine.

'She should be thankful, Mammy and I raised you while she was flying around the world instead of taking care of you herself,' Uncle Pierre said, with venom in his voice.

'She's thankful, very thankful. And she's told me this repeatedly over the years. But what does that have anything to do with the way you react about the medals?'

'Because it's typical of her behaviour. That she can simply roll up and always get what she wants.'

'That's completely ridiculous. It makes absolutely no sense. She's only asked for two things, and you went berserk. No flexibility on your part.' Max took a sip of his scotch.

Silence.

'She's the first to recognise that she stuffed up when she was young. I'm fully aware of it. Trust me I know. Mistakes can't be turned back but she has more than tried to atone for the errors of her youth. And, yes, she was lucky to have her family to help her out during those difficult times. So let it go, move on and give her a break.

Silence.

'Please do it for me. I'm going back to Australia in a couple of days, and it would make me very sad to know that she went back to the US on this sour note.' Max finished his scotch. 'Please make up. You'd really regret it if you don't.'

'Okay, let me think about it.'

'Thank you. I appreciate it.'

Max got up. 'I've got to go. I've got a few things to do. Putting aside this fight, it was good to catch up after all those years and to finally meet you, Jeannette.'

They got up as well. Max shook hands with Uncle Pierre, they gave each other a hug, and he gave Jeannette three kisses on the cheeks.

'Let's try not to wait twenty years to meet again,' Max said, with a cheeky grin. 'It's clearly not good.'

6

Mwadui – Janet (1972)

The wildebeests stretched as far as the eye could see. Millions of them. Like a massive river, they were flowing and undulating over the landscape, as one body, with nothing stopping them on their long journey through the Serengeti. It was mesmerising. From where I was perched, I had the best possible view of the wonderful spectacle that had been repeated millions of times back to the very beginning of dawn.

I was sitting in the jump seat in the cockpit of the DC-3 flying us from Nairobi to Mwadui, about 500 km southeast of Lake Victoria in Tanzania. John was the captain.

Mwadui was the site of the Williamson Diamond Mine, probably the biggest open-pit diamond mine outside of South Africa. It was established in 1940 after a Canadian geologist, Dr John Williamson, discovered the site. A small community of expatriates, some 50 families, mainly from the UK, lived in Mwadui. John had been hired as one of the four pilots in Mwadui about a year earlier.

I leaned over and said to John, 'I love Africa. It's so majestic, so vast, so raw.'

He turned his head and smiled, 'I know, that's what I love about it too.'

I really looked forward to this short one-hour plane trip during which we flew over the Serengeti across the

Rift Valley and Peter's Pond. Seeing all those hundreds of thousands of wild animals was so spectacular.

But there was one thing I looked forward to even more and that was to see Janet again. I hadn't seen her in six months since Christmas 1971 when I first met her. We immediately fell in love, as sixteen-year-olds tend to do. We had written to each other often over the past six months. I so looked forward to receiving her letters. And when I got one from her and one from Mum on the same day at boarding school, I had hit the jackpot.

'I'm going to go and see Mum. I'll be back for the landing,' I said to John.

'Sure, we should be arriving in about 20 minutes.'

There were a dozen passengers on board, many of them looking out of the windows to admire the beauty of the scenery. Mum was sitting in the front row. I sat in the vacant aisle seat next to her. She too was looking out the window.

'Isn't it beautiful?'

'Oh, darling! I hadn't seen you come out of the cockpit.'

'It's so good to be coming back to Mwadui.'

'It's great to have you here with us for two months. We miss you so much each time you go back to boarding school.' She squeezed my hand.

'I can't wait to see Janet and my other friends. They'll all be there at the hangar waiting.'

'It's so nice how people do this here. Waiting for the plane to arrive to welcome people home.'

'I know. I suppose there's not much else to do, really. By the way, do you mind if we give Janet a ride back to our house?'

'Of course, I don't mind.'

I looked out of the window.

'I can't wait to see Claudia in two weeks when she comes to visit,' I said.

'Neither can I. And to all go on safari together will be so much fun.'

'I know. It'll be so exciting.'

Our conversation was interrupted by John making his usual announcement, 'Ladies and gentlemen, this is your captain speaking. We'll be arriving in about ten minutes, so please return to your seats and fasten your seatbelt, ensure your seat is in its upright position, and extinguish all cigarettes for our final approach to Mwadui International Airport.'

'He loves adding the international to his broadcast,' I said.

'I know. It tickles him. You'd better get back in the cockpit if you want to be there for the landing.'

'Okay, I'll see you later.'

Back in the cockpit, I could see on the horizon the diamond mine. As we got closer to Mwadui, John tipped the starboard wing so that all the passengers on the right could have a good view of the scenery and then he repeated the manoeuvre for the other side as he prepared for his approach to the airport. John always made it a point to make impeccable landings. And this time he did it again. We hardly felt the touch down even though it was a dirt strip.

As soon as the back-cargo door of the DC-3 was opened, I saw Janet standing there by the hangar with other friends. As I started walking towards her, I saw that she was exactly how I expected her to look. She was wearing a light-yellow summer dress, with the hem mid-thigh. No bra. My heart was pounding as I got closer to her. Her shoulder-length blond hair was flying in the sun-drenched breeze. She walked forward and our lips met tenderly and softly. We wanted to keep the hungry kissing for later, away from everyone else's prying eyes.

'So good to see you, darling,' she said.

'Great to be here and finally kiss you, sweetheart.'

'I'm wearing your favourite colour,' she said.

'I know. I noticed right away from the plane. You're so gorgeous.'

We held hands and walked back to the other members of the welcoming party. There must have been about a dozen people. Jake, a 6'4" Canadian, was there, as was Judy, another Canadian. We all had a good laugh and arranged to meet the next day at the swimming pool.

In the back of the Land Rover, Janet and I were sitting very close to each other, so close that our thighs touched. John was driving and Mum was in the passenger seat in front. I ran my hand along Janet's inner thigh under the hem of her dress, caressing delicately the soft skin, out of Mum's line of vision.

'I can't wait to caress you everywhere,' I whispered quietly in her ear.

'Nor can I.'

'It's so great to be back home,' I said, for the benefit of all in the Land Rover, winking at Janet.

'It's great to have you back,' John said.

We drove for about ten minutes along the double 10-foot-high wire mesh fence which surrounded the whole perimeter of the diamond mine.

When we finally got home, Benson and Souku, our staff members, were waiting for me.

'Welcome home, Bwana,' they both said in unison.

'Thank you so much. It's great to be back and to see you both. Really is.' As I said that, I shook their hands and held their hands with my left hand.

'And how's your little boy Benson?'

'He's growing very quick, Bwana.'

'You must bring him to the house one of these days so I can see him.'

'I will, sir, thank you.'

'And how's your mother Souku?'

'She's much better, Sir.'

'That's great to hear that.'

'You probably want to be alone,' Mum said.

'Actually, we would. Would you mind terribly if we escaped to my bedroom?' I asked, smiling.

'Of course not. I'm sure you have a lot of catching up to do.'

'Thank you, Mum,' as I gave her a big hug.

Janet and I went to the very back of the house to my bedroom. We entered the room, and I shut the door behind us.

****

'Who's the woman with the two young kids?' I asked Jake, pointing at the far end of the swimming pool.

We were all sitting around on our towels on the grass at one end of the swimming pool area. The sun was shining, no wind. A perfect sunny summer afternoon in Tanzania. There must have been about 10 of us, the number kept changing depending on who was coming and going. From where we were camped out, we could see the tee-off for hole number three of the very basic golf course, just on the other side of the fence.

'That's Françoise. She and her husband Jean-Pierre arrived about four months ago. They're from France. He's a geologist,' Jake said. 'She's very friendly.'

'I'll have to meet her one day.'

'So, how's boarding school been?' Jake asked.

'Fine. I'm sure happy another year bites the dust. Only two more to go and finished with boarding school. I wish I could do the studying by correspondence like you and be here enjoying the nice weather.'

'Actually, it's not as much fun as you think. It's difficult to get motivated. There's no one to answer questions. And because of the mail system, it takes at least three weeks to get a response to things,' Jake said.

'But at least you're with other Canadian friends who can help out, like Judy here,' I said, turning to her.

'That's exactly right,' Judy said, joining in the conversation. 'There's enough of us to be able to have productive study periods together. I sure wouldn't want to be doing that alone in the bush.'

'Yeah, that would be awful on so many levels,' I said.

'I'm going for a swim,' Jake said. A couple of others joined him. As was his wont, he went straight to the top diving board and threw himself into the pool rolled up in a ball. He thought it was the funniest thing to do, but everyone else thought it was annoying, especially the ones who got drenched.

'I see you're reading The Drifters. I read it a couple of months ago,' I said to Judy. 'What do you think of it?'

'I like it. It would have to be so much fun travelling around Europe and North Africa like the characters in the novel do.'

'It would have,' I said. I looked around and saw that the French woman had gone with her two children to the kids' wading pool at the very far end of the swimming pool area.

'You know, I learned in that book that the Beatles' song Lucy in the Sky with Diamonds actually refers to LSD. Did you know that?' I said.

'I didn't know that either. But I suppose it makes sense given the lyrics of the song!'

'Yes, really!'

'Speaking of reading, I might do a bit of reading myself,' I said, taking out a book from my satchel.

'What are you reading?' Judy asked.

'"Uhuru" by Robert Ruark. It's really great. John recommended it.'

'I think I've seen it around. What's it about?'

'It's about the independence of Kenya and the lead-up to it. He really captures it well. The divisions, the hatred, the violence.'

'Can I see?' she asked.

'Sure,' as I gave her the book to look at.

'I'm going to get a Coke while you look at it. Anybody want anything from the shopfront?'

When I got to the store, Françoise and her two children were in front of me, waiting in line.

'Vous voulez une glace les enfants?' she asked the children.

'Je suis certain que oui,' I said, loud enough for her to hear me.

Clearly surprised to hear French, she turned around. 'Est ce que j'entends un petit accent belge?'

And that's when I saw her eyes for the first time. Françoise had the most unforgettable, unique emerald green eyes, piercing and beautiful at the same time. Quite simply mesmerizing.

'Is it that obvious?' I asked, still trying to take in the beauty of her eyes.

'Just a bit, but nothing to be worried about. It's cute,' she said, with a big smile.

'That's reassuring.'

'I haven't seen you around.'

'Sorry, I should have introduced myself. I'm Michel. I'm John and Juliette's son. John is one of the pilots. He's the American one. I arrived yesterday from Belgium where I go to boarding school.'

'I'm Françoise. We only arrived a few months ago. My husband is one of the geologists.'

'Pleased to meet you,' I said, as we shook hands.

Looking at me, she said, 'Yes, of course, I can now see the family resemblance with your mother Juliette. We speak in French as well when we meet.'

The line had moved forward, and she was now at the counter.

'Alors, les enfants. Vous avez décidé ce que vous voulez?' she asked the children.

Once she and the kids had their ice creams, they moved away from the counter. I got my Coke. They were waiting for me as I was making my way back to my friends.

'I'm sure we'll meet again soon,' she said.

'Certainement. C'était un plaisir.'

'I just had a chat with Françoise and her kids. She seems very nice,' I said, as I settled down on my towel.

'Yes, she's very nice,' Judy said. 'By the way, could I borrow your book when you're finished with it? It looks really good.'

'Of course, you can.'

Janet finally arrived. She was wearing the cutest red bikini. Her top covered firm, well-proportioned breasts which I had fondled, kissed, licked, caressed, nibbled and pinched most lovingly the evening before. She placed her towel right against mine and then lay down on her tummy next to me, actually snuggled up to me. I could feel her thigh against mine. It was so pleasant to have her so close to me. Life was good.

****

By the time I got to the party, Santana's "Black Magic Woman" was blaring away. It had an incredibly catchy beat to it which drew people to the dance floor. This was closely followed by Deep Purple's "Smoke on the Water", another favourite of all. Lots of bass. Lots of beat. Lots of fun.

Jonathan's party was going very well. Jonathan was one of those guys who was friends with everyone. He had parents who were relaxed about having parties at their house. So much so that most parties were held at his house. Most people suspected that his parents smoked weed on a regular basis. The living room had been stripped of everything, leaving only the minimum furniture required. The rest was dance floor space. The only lighting was coming from the kitchen. As we were all underage, no alcohol was officially allowed, but everyone had brought their stash of booze and had hidden it in various parts of the garden.

Janet arrived at the party with a couple of her girlfriends. She was wearing the yellow dress. She only wore it for special occasions.

'You look beautiful love,' I said, as I kissed her softly on the lips.

'You don't look too bad yourself.'

We danced for a couple of hours or so, including on Rare Earth's "Get Ready" which went on for almost half an hour. We managed to sneak down a couple of shots of scotch from the bottle Jack had hidden in the back garden. He only shared it with a select few.

'Let's get out of here and have some fun. I have a surprise for you,' Janet whispered in my ear, trying to make herself heard over the din of the music.

'That's a great idea. I thought you'd never ask.'

Everyone was too busy doing their own thing to notice our departure. We went straight across the road and walked onto the golf course. The full moon was so bright that it made it easy to find our way to the small grassy mound by hole four. It was our favourite spot partially hidden by bushes on one side. We lay down and began to kiss and fondle each other with passion, as if for the first time.

'Michel, I want to go all the way tonight.'

'Really? Is it safe?'

'Yes, I checked, and it will be safe.'

'Oh, love. I was hoping this day would come soon.' I held her tightly in my arms. 'I've never gone all the way.'

The Green Elevator Cage

'Neither have I. We'll just have to see how we go, won't we, darling?' she said, with a warm smile on her face.

The next twenty minutes were a mix of fumbling, fondling, exploring, laughing, caressing, tenderness and lots of loving. We were virgins, and we were kids discovering together one of life's great pleasures. Time stopped.

Lying on our backs, we looked at the stars.

'I'm sorry I didn't perform so well,' I said, holding her hand tightly.

'Don't be silly, Michel. It was our first go at it. I know we'll improve with time and get the hang of it.'

'I love you so much, Janet.'

'I know. I do too. That's why I wanted you to be the first one. And you know what they say, you never forget your first one. So, you're safe in my memory forever, darling.'

We were still lying on our backs. The night air was balmy. Looking at the moon, it looked so close, it felt we could almost touch it.

'It always amazes me how many more stars there are in the southern hemisphere, or at least appears to be. It's like being under a massive dome. Can you identify the various constellations because I can't?' I said.

'Neither can I.'

Silence.

'Funny to think that I was born in Mwadui and now I've just made love with you. And you were born on the other side of the continent.'

'I know, it's crazy.'

Silence.

'Do you want to go back to the party?' I asked, without much enthusiasm. Although we were quite a long way from it, we could faintly hear the music.

'Not really, Michel. I don't want to ruin our beautiful moment with more loud music. I'd rather go home.'

'Neither do I. I'll walk you back.'

We got up and, holding hands, we walked slowly to Janet's house, stopping often to kiss passionately. When we got to her house, we sat on the front stairs.

'It was such a beautiful evening, Janet. One I will never forget, ever.'

'Neither will I.'

I started to caress her, softly touching her braless breasts, teasing her nipples which had slightly hardened with the cool air.

'I think you'd better stop now sweetheart because I know exactly where you are heading,' she said, tapping the tip of my nose with her index finger.

'Yes, but it's fun.'

'I know, but not now. We'll have plenty of opportunities when we all go on safari in two weeks,' she said.

'Okay, you're right love. I'd better head off.'

As I walked home to the sound of millions of crickets after dropping Janet at her house, I looked at the bright moon and thought, yes, life is indeed very good. And, even better, Claudia would be visiting us very soon.

****

'It's so great to have Claudia visiting us here in Mwadui,' I said to Mum, sitting next to her in the DC-3. 'She must love being in the cockpit with John.'

'I'm sure she's enjoying it a lot, especially seeing all the roaming animals.'

'She looked so happy to see us as she came down the plane stairs in Nairobi,' I said.

'Yes, she sure did.'

'I can't wait to introduce her to Janet, Jack and the others when we go to the swimming pool tomorrow.'

'Yes, that should be fun.'

We both looked outside to have a view of the great scenery unfurling below us and the hundreds and thousands of animals roving the Serengeti plains. Each time I saw this magnificent spectacle I was in total awe.

'Mum, now that I have you to myself, I've been meaning to ask you. Have you had a chance to talk to my father about his very long silence?'

She looked outside.

'Mum, could you please look at me?'

After a long interval, she turned her head around. 'No, Michel, I haven't been in touch with him as I said I would. I'm sorry.'

'But why? You promised me and Claudia you would. That was over two years ago.'

'I know I did, but I can't get myself to get in touch with him. It brings back too many bad memories.'

'You know what? I'm tired of waiting for you or him for that matter to get things moving. When I get back to Brussels I might just go and pay him a visit. I'll organise something with Claudia.'

'No, Michel, I'll get in touch with him, and then I'll let you know the outcome. What do you think of that?'

'Is that a promise?'

We could hear John giving his usual spiel just before landing. So, we buckled up.

'Yes, it's a promise.'

'Thank you, Mum. I really appreciate it. You know I love you so much.'

'I know Michel. And I love you too, lots,' as she squeezed my hand.

****

'So how long are you going to be visiting us?' Judy asked Claudia.

The usual crowd was sitting around on the grass by the swimming pool. I had brought Claudia with me. It was yet again a beautiful sunny day with only a few small lost clouds sprinkled high in the sky.

'For about three weeks,' Claudia said.

'That's great,' said Judy.

'I can't wait to go on safari next week,' I said. 'It should be so much fun.'

Almost in unison Janet, Judy and Jake all said, 'That will be so cool.'

We were all going to be part of a safari that our parents had been organising for months. We would be gone for a week. We were all looking forward to it.

'It's so crazy that we only have to go out the gate, drive a few hours and we'll be in the middle of millions of animals. People would pay thousands of dollars in the US or Europe to be able to do that,' I said to the group.

'That's so right,' Jake said.

'So where did you pick up your excellent English, Claudia?' Judy asked.

'I was an au pair in London for one year recently. That's where I really learned it.'

'Why don't you live in Belgium like Michel does?' Jake asked.

'It's a bit complicated but basically, it's because when we were very young our parents divorced. We were then living in the Belgian Congo. Our father took me, and our mother got Michel. That's why we didn't see that much of each other over the years.'

'That's very sad,' said Janet.

Janet was lying next to me, as usual, snuggled up to me.

'Yes, it's very sad. But now that we are older, we can more easily visit each other.'

'So, have you lived in exotic places like Saudi Arabia and Beirut as Michel has?'

'No, I haven't been as lucky as my brother. I've been stuck in Zurich my whole life, except of course for London.'

I could see in the far corner of the swimming pool area Françoise and her children. It looked like she was reading them a story from a book and showing them pictures. She was wearing a yellow bikini made of some sort of crochet material. She looked very attractive.

'So, were you both born in the Congo?' Jake asked.

'Yes, but Claudia was born in Elizabethville, now called Lubumbashi and I was born in Leopoldville, now called Kinshasa,' I said.

'Wow, that's so exotic,' Jake said, with a broad smile on his face.

'Have you been back since you left?' Judy asked.

'I haven't but Michel was back in Kinshasa last year,' Claudia said.

'That's right. And it's now so run down. It's awful. The city must have been beautiful and well-maintained at the time of independence but now it's looking pretty decrepit. I hate to think what the city will look like twenty or thirty years from now.'

'I think we've asked you enough questions,' Judy said. 'Time for a swim.'

'Great idea. I thought we'd never go in!' Claudia said.

****

'Let's wait until it stops raining and then we can go to the community centre and check the mail,' I said to Claudia.

We were standing on the front veranda of our house protected from the tons of water coming down from the heavens. There was literally a wall of water blocking our view and our path to our transportation.

'Does it often rain like this?'

'At this time of the year, every day. Almost always at about the same time, around 5 pm. The downpour lasts only ten minutes,' I shouted, so loud was the din of the rain falling on the tin roof. 'I just love these buckets of rain. It's so fantastic, so powerful.'

'It is exciting,' she said.

When the rain finally subsided, we jumped into the Land Rover. I had only recently learned to drive. So, I looked for any excuse to get behind the wheel.

The arrival of the mail was a big event in Mwadui. The mail came with the weekly flight from Nairobi, and everyone knew the arrival time of the flight. We gave the postal service an hour to get the mailbags from the airport and start distributing the mail in the individual postal boxes. We all waited eagerly in clusters for the postal clerk to distribute the mail. It was an opportunity to catch up with people and share some gossip. I could see as we approached the congregation that Françoise was also waiting with her two children. It gave me a frisson.

'Bonjour Françoise,' I said.

'Ah, bonjour Michel, Comment ça va?'

'Very well. Can I introduce you to my sister, Claudia? She's visiting us.'

They shook hands.

'I can see the family resemblance. But the accent is this time not Belgian but Swiss,' she said, slightly surprised.

'You're right, but it's too long to explain right now,' I said.

'How long are you visiting for?' Françoise asked as she was trying to manage her two children who were running around trying to catch each other.

'Only three weeks,' Claudia said.

'We're off on a safari next week. So that should be lots of fun,' I said.

'It will be. I'm sure. We need to do one of those as well but with two little children it's not so easy as you can well imagine,' she said, still trying to control her children.

'How have you been? I see you bring the children to the swimming pool every day,' I asked.

'I've been fine. Jean-Pierre is often gone for days on geological trips looking for more diamond sources. So, I look after the kids and bring them to the pool in the afternoon after daycare in the morning. They love it.'

'I'm sure. They are a bit of a handful, I see.'

'I think the mail has arrived,' she said, looking at the postal boxes being filled with letters from the inside by the postal clerk.

Once we had collected our mail, we bade goodbye to Françoise and hopped back into the Land Rover. I started the engine and drove out of the car park.

'I've been meaning to tell you about the conversation I had with Mum on the plane coming down from Nairobi now that we finally have a bit of time alone.'

'Oh, yes, tell me.'

'Well, in a nutshell, Mum has done nothing. She never called or wrote to our father as she said she would.'

'That doesn't really surprise me because if she had, I'm sure father would have said something to me. Or maybe not, I don't know anymore.'

Silence.

I had decided to take the long way back home. So now we were driving along a hard dirt track that hugged the mine's perimeter security fence.

'You know lately, and maybe I should have thought about this earlier, but the more I think about it the more I think that our father may not be my father after all. And his silence would explain it,' I said.

Silence.

'What do you think?' quickly looking over to Claudia.

'It had crossed my mind as well Michel, actually a number of times, but I didn't want to suggest it before you had come to this possibility yourself.'

'You know, the more I think about it, the more I think that can be the only explanation for his silence.'

'But why the silence by both?' Claudia asked.

'Maybe they think we'll just forget about it, or that this issue will simply go away by itself. Which of course it won't.'

Silence.

We had arrived home. I parked the Land Rover in the driveway. But neither one of us made any move to get out.

'I think it may be because it may be too painful for your father to talk about it. And that's why when you have asked him, he has repeatedly said that he doesn't want to talk about it.'

'It does start to make sense,' Claudia said.

'But why doesn't Mum just tell us?'

'You know, Michel, it could be that she's embarrassed and maybe ashamed that she got pregnant by another man while married to my father.'

'Quite possibly.'

Silence.

'But she's going to have to tell me, us, what's the truth,' I said.

'I know.'

'I simply can never find the right moment to talk to her about this. And she certainly never makes it easy for us to approach her about this.'

'That's for sure.'

'And you know, only seeing Mum once a year during the summer holidays makes it even more difficult.'

Mum came out of the house, very obviously looking for us.

'Ah, there you are. I thought I'd heard the Land Rover.'

'We were just having a bit of a chat Mum,' I said.

Turning to Claudia, 'We can continue this conversation later,' I said in a low voice, as I squeezed her hand and winked before opening the car door.

'There's lots of mail Mum,' I said.

****

The big day had finally arrived. We'd agreed to meet at the front gate at 6 am so we could have an early start for the four-hundred-kilometre road trip to Lobo Lodge in the middle of Serengeti National Park. The caravan was made up of four vehicles, which in addition to us consisted of three other families, Janet's, Jake's and Judy's. Although the distance we had to travel wasn't that long, the road conditions were poor, and a substantial part of the travel was in the park itself which meant that our average speed was about sixty km an hour. Still, it was lots of fun to be doing this with Claudia. And to have Janet with us made it extra special.

Lobo Lodge was a great place to stop for three days. It had been built on a rocky outcrop. The view of the Serengeti Plain from an impressive viewing deck was spectacular, with a whole array of roaming animals, like giraffes, hartebeests, zebras and gazelles, that could be seen in the distance. Not far from the deck below, a watering hole attracted animals all day long as well as at night, when it was lit with powerful spotlights enabling visitors to see cheetahs, lions and hyenas coming to quench their thirst.

However, neither the beauty of the scenery nor the amazing wildlife could stop me from paying more attention to Janet. This did not impress John, not that he ever told me. It was Mum who would tell me.

'Michel, John feels you are not paying enough attention to the wildlife and too much attention to Janet instead,' she said to me one day.

'You are joking, right?'

'No, he's serious.'

'Well, in that case, let him tell me himself. I think I'm able to look at the zillions of wildebeest and Janet at the same time.'

'Just humour him a bit, please. Don't forget that this is also his fortieth birthday present, so this safari has a special significance for him.'

'It's ridiculous. But sure. I'll look at the stripes on the zebras more closely.'

'Oh Michel, you know what I mean.'

'No, I don't. But for you, I'll show more enthusiasm for the wildlife.'

But Janet and I didn't care, so at any opportunity we would sneak away from the group and find a discreet place where we could spend some time alone kissing and fondling each other. We could never have enough of each other. But I also wanted to spend time with Claudia and not give the impression that I was abandoning her. However, she didn't seem to mind my absence too much, having found a kindred spirit with Brian, Janet's 20-year-old brother. Having recently visited Europe, including Switzerland, Brian was keen to share notes with Claudia. So, all in all, it looked like everyone was happy with the situation, except perhaps John.

After three days at the Lodge, the caravan was back on the road, and we went camping for four days in a pre-designated place not too far away. That was lots of fun, with the tents all installed in a semi-circle around the large campfire. In the evenings we would all gather around the fire, exchange stories of the day's events, and the various animals we had seen and eat our barbequed meal. Janet and I always sat together and, if possible, we would try to sneak out, but it was rather conspicuous when we weren't there. Lovemaking was out of the question, as was visiting each other in the middle of the night as she was sharing a tent with her mother, and I was sharing one with John. At night, in our tents, we could hear the animals move about close to the tent and roam rather loudly. The campfire helped keep potential predators away as did a patrolling park scout.

Sadly, after four days of camping in the middle of the Serengeti surrounded by millions of amazing animals in a breathless environment, the fun had to stop, and we had to return to Mwadui.

'Hey, Brian, would you terribly mind switching places with me for the trip back so I can be with Janet? That way you could also be Claudia,' I asked Brian, as we were all packing up early in the morning for the six-hour trip back.

'Not at all, mate. But are your parents okay with that?'

'Yeah, they are perfectly fine with that.' Little did he know that I had only asked Mum for the switch, and only a few minutes earlier. John would be faced with a fait accompli, but he'd be too busy driving to care too much. Claudia would be quite pleased to be able to spend some time with Brian. We would have other opportunities to talk. The road trip back was uneventful, but it was bliss to be able to simply sit in the back with Janet, holding hands and enjoying the beautiful fauna and flora for most of the trip back.

The Green Elevator Cage

****

A few days after our return from our safari, Claudia and I were sitting in the living room chatting when John announced to us that he had to make an unexpected trip to Lubumbashi the next day to pick up some heavy mining equipment.

'Would you be interested in coming along? It's about 1200 kilometres away so the trip will take about three hours each way in the DC-4.'

We looked at each other in total disbelief. Without having to talk about it, in unison we said we'd love to do the trip.

'I thought so,' John said.

'It would be so great to see where I was born and where my life started,' she said.

'Well, then it's a deal. We leave the house at 5 am.'

'Thank you so much for taking us, John. It'll mean a lot to Claudia and me to be able to be back in the Congo together,' I said. 'But what about Mum? I'm sure she'd love to come too and see Elizabethville.'

'I've already asked her, and she said she'd prefer to remember the city she's got such great memories of as it was when she left, not the way it is now.'

'I can understand that,' I said.

The flight was long and not very comfortable.

'It must feel strange to think that soon you'll be setting foot where you were born,' I said to Claudia, who was sitting next to me on one of only two seats in the whole plane.

The hull of the plane had been configured to transport cargo, not passengers.

'Yes, very strange Michel. To think it all started here in 1953. It will feel like it's not really about me but someone else.'

'You're probably right. I suspect it'll look very different from how it did nineteen years ago. Probably very run down.'

'I'm sure you are right,' she said.

'I know that when I went to Kinshasa last year, it felt very foreign to me. But not completely because of all the stories I had heard and pictures I had seen over the years.'

We had to almost shout because of the noise of the engines and the emptiness of the cabin.

'I'm so happy we can do this together. That we can go back to the Congo where our lives started and where we were separated,' she said.

'I know it's great. We're very lucky that it just so happened that John had to fly to Lubumbashi. Life can throw such funny things at you.'

'Michel, I've been waiting for the best moment to give you this small present I brought with me from Zurich. And I think this is a really good one.' Claudia dug into the satchel she had brought with her and pulled out a small package.

'I wonder what it is?'

'Open it, you'll see then!'

I opened the carefully wrapped package, and it revealed a silver cigarette lighter on which were engraved on one of the sides, the following words, "For my little brother. Always your sister. xxx Claudia".

'That's so, so beautiful Claudia! I will treasure this with my life forever.'

'I'm so happy you like it that much.'

The Green Elevator Cage

'It's great. And so unexpected.' We hugged each other.

'But I won't be able to use it in Mwadui because Mum and John don't yet know that I smoke. I'll have to find the right moment to tell them.'

'Of course, don't worry about it. I really quite understand.'

I kissed it and I put it in my pocket. I was so touched by that present. I took Claudia's hand, squeezed it, and we smiled at each other.

We regularly paid visits to John and his co-pilot in the cockpit. He would tell us where we were and show us various landmarks. Once we had crossed over into the Congo the scenery changed, and the vegetation became much lusher and dense. The only thing we could see then was the canopy of the dense forest below. So, we went back to our two seats to talk some more. An hour or so later, we landed in Lubumbashi.

'It looks like it could take up to three hours to load the equipment we came for, so why don't we go into town and check it out?' John said as we were waiting in the dilapidated airport terminal.

'That's a great idea,' Claudia said, trying to take in her unfamiliar surroundings.

'But let's first get a bite to eat,' I suggested.

'Yes, let's do that,' John said.

'Hey boss, taxi?' shouted a local man at the wheel of a beat-up Peugeot 404. He had a massive smile from ear to ear and about fifty-six teeth. The car had obviously seen the wars. The car's antenna was an upside-down metal coat hanger precariously holding to dear life where the original antenna used to live. 'I bring you anywhere in Lubumbashi. I know all.'

We looked at each other and John said, 'Okay. Let's take this one.' John jumped in front with the driver, and I went in the back with Claudia. The backseat had a major rip across it like an open wound that had never healed. There were no seat belts.

'Hotel Belle Vue please,' John said to the driver.

'Ah good choice!' the driver said. 'Best hotel.'

Lubumbashi was run down, dirty, busy and dusty. Having looked at family pictures of the city around the time of independence, one could hardly recognise it was the same city. It was absolutely a shadow of its former self. John, who had spent some time there shortly after independence, confirmed that in ten years the city had degraded significantly. Claudia was shocked, but then she hadn't been back to Africa since the mid-1950s. It took about 20 minutes to drive from the airport to the hotel. Hotel Belle Vue had been built some thirty years earlier by Italians and had become a major city landmark ever since. Claudia was silent, trying to take in the rawness of the environment. We had lunch at the restaurant in the hotel which tried its best to maintain standards when everything around it was fast crumbling.

Sitting on the veranda, having our lunch, I said, 'It's so great to be here to see where Mum lived when she was young. Thank you so much John for taking us with you.' I took a sip of my Coke.

'Yes, it's so great to see where I was born,' Claudia said.

'Speaking of which, I thought we could check out the hospital where you were born. It's less than a kilometre from here. We could walk to it and from there take a taxi back to the airport,' John said.

Beggars, mainly children, tried to reach up to sell us trinkets and other useless and worthless small plastic items.

'Isn't it sad that these poor kids have to try to sell these things,' Claudia said.

'It's very sad, but there's nothing we can do,' John said.

'Can we buy something from them as a souvenir?' she asked.

'Of course, we can,' John said.

She leaned over the railing, examining the various items in a basket which the smallest of the children, probably no more than seven years old, was struggling to hold up so she could look at what was for sale.

'I'd like that,' she said, pointing to a small, black wooden elephant with little beady eyes made of bits of ivory. John pulled out a wad of local notes.

'Please don't bargain with the little boy. His whole family probably depends on this. Just give him what he asks,' she said.

'Okay, Claudia.' John paid the young boy and gave Claudia the little elephant.

'Thank you, John. I really appreciate it. I will always treasure this little elephant as a souvenir of our trip to my homeland,' she said, with a beautiful smile.

We continued our lunch, mainly in silence, looking at the passing traffic of people and cars negotiating the roundabout in front of the hotel. It was mesmerising to see all the movement in front of us. Claudia took many pictures of us and the city with her Kodak 104. I had one as well, but I had forgotten to take it with me.

'Time is moving on. We better go now and see the hospital. It's not very far, so we can go on foot,' John said. 'That way we can get a better sense of the city.'

It took us fifteen minutes to get there, walking straight down avenues Kasai and Munongo. There wasn't much to see, just a lot of run-down shops selling goods of all types. There were quite a few other expatriates milling about doing their shopping.

When we got to the Clinique Universitaire, one of the oldest hospitals originally established by the Belgians, Claudia got all excited.

'I can't believe this is where it all started.'

'It's incredible,' I said, as I reached for her hand and squeezed it.

'I never thought I'd ever see this place, and with you as well Michel. What a very, very special occasion. I'll never forget this moment. Never.'

We walked around a bit. Like the rest of Lubumbashi, the hospital was very rundown. The humidity had generated dark mildew everywhere, the paint was peeling off, parts of the roof were broken, and weeds were growing everywhere. It was a very sad sight. Still, Claudia took lots of pictures.

'I want to capture this moment forever.'

'We better go now,' John said, not really wanting to interrupt our reunion with our mother's past.

'Yes, you are right,' I said.

John flagged down a taxi, one that also had an upside-down metal coat hanger as an antenna. It seemed de rigueur in this town. We were at the airport in less than 20 minutes. The plane had been loaded up and was ready for departure. The co-pilot was waiting for us, having supervised the loading of the heavy machinery.

When we were finally sitting in our two seats and we had levelled off after taking off, I turned to Claudia.

'Wasn't that just great!'

'It was so great Michel. I will always treasure this short, unplanned trip to the Congo. What a very special thing!'

'Speaking of the past, I don't think this is a good time to talk to Mum about my father, whoever he may be. You only have a couple of days left in Mwadui and we don't want to upset her unnecessarily. I'm sure we'll find an opportunity down the road. What do you think?'

'I think you're right Michel. We can wait. And I'm sure she'd also be happy to wait,' she said, with a grin on her face.

'Thank you,' as I squeezed her hand.

Mum, wearing a colourful summer dress, was waiting for us on the veranda when we got back. She was sitting in a wicker chair with a glass of martini.

'Oh Mum, it was so great to see where I was born!' Claudia said with great enthusiasm.

'I knew you'd love to go and see where it all started,' she said, as she hugged us in turn.

'It would have been great if we could have shared this together,' I said.

'I know Michel. But I preferred not to go and instead live on the wonderful memories I have of the place.'

'I understand perfectly.'

'Well, I think I need a good wash after this long trip across Africa!' Claudia said. Turning to John, 'And again, thank you so much for doing this for us.'

'Yes, thank you heaps.'
'You are both most welcome. It was fun.'

****

Sadly, the day had arrived when Claudia had to leave. We all went to the airport, but I wasn't going to be accompanying her to Nairobi. John would be flying the DC-3 and Mum would go up with him. They would be back in Mwadui around 6 pm.

It was 6 am. The air was crisp and fresh, promising a beautiful new day.

'Well, that's it then, the sad moment has arrived,' I said to Claudia, as we hugged each other at the foot of the metal steps going up to the plane. John was already in the cockpit doing his pre-flight check. Mum had already gone into the plane.

'Oh Michel, it was such a great experience to come here, to have long chats, meet your friends, go on safari and, of course, to go to Lubumbashi. What a holiday!'

'I know. It was full-on. Lots of fun. I'm so sorry you have to go but I'll be in touch when I get back to Brussels. We can organise a time for me to visit you in Zurich.'

'Yes, you must come and visit me,' she said.

'But the more I think about it, I think I should pass on seeing your father then because I think you are right.'

'I'm sorry Michel, but I think there's somebody else involved in this whole business,' she said.

'Regardless, I love you lots, and you will always be my sister.'

'Same here. You will always be my little brother!' she said, with the sweetest smile.

We hugged once more, and then she went up the metal staircase. We waved each other goodbye as she entered the plane.

I got into the Land Rover and drove straight to Janet's house. She was expecting me.

'How did it go, Michel?' Janet asked as she opened the front door.

'It was sad to see her go. We had such a good time while she was here. I was so happy to be able to share Africa with her. An important thing we have in common.'

'I know what you mean.'

'I thought we could spend most of the day at my place, and maybe go the pool if we felt like it.'

'That sounds great.'

When we got home, we went straight to my bedroom. She quite naturally, without any inhibition, took off all her clothes, revealing her most beautiful, tanned and proportioned body. She promptly jumped into the bed.

'Well darling, don't just stand there. What are you waiting for? The girl is keen.'

I stripped off.

'Good to see you are just as keen.'

We made love all morning, taking breaks to make some coffee or have a bite to eat.

'It's good to see you've lifted your game since the first time,' she said, poking a finger in my rib as we were laying on the bed naked.

'Thank you. So have you incidentally,' I said, as I rolled over to kiss her right nipple tenderly.

'Darling, I'm so going to miss these beautiful moments together when I'll be back in miserable, rainy UK.'

'I know what you mean. It rains a lot in Belgium as well,' I said to try to lighten the moment. 'But I'll come to visit you in England.'

'I know you will and that'll be great. But I also know that it won't be the same. Not at all.

Silence.

'We won't have the warmth. The privacy. The sound of the birds. The smell of Africa. None of that,' she said.

'Sweetheart, you mustn't think about all that. Let's go to the pool for a couple of hours and then come back for more playing.'

'You're right Michel. Let's do that,' she leaned over and kissed me softly on the lips.

'Where have you guys been?' Judy asked as soon as she saw us approach the usual gang at the pool.

I ignored the question.

'Another beautiful day in sunny Tanzania,' I said. As I was putting down my towel on the grass, I saw that Françoise was with her two children at the usual far end of the swimming pool area. Janet laid her towel right next to mine as always.

About an hour later, I saw that Françoise had gone to the shopfront. I got up and asked if anyone wanted anything from the shopfront.

'Bonjour Françoise,' I said.

'Ah, bonjour Michel. Comment ça va?'

Her green eyes drew me into her world. I suspect she knew it too.

'All good here. Except that, my sister Claudia left early this morning.'

'I'm sorry to hear. She seems like a very nice girl.'

The Green Elevator Cage

'She is. We are close even though we've been separated most of our lives.'

'That often happens actually.'

'And to make things worse, Janet is leaving in a couple of days.'

'Who is Janet? Your girlfriend?'

Françoise was struggling to control her two children who were running around the area. She had absolutely no control over them.

'Yes, she is.'

After I got my Coke, I said goodbye.

'I'm sure we'll meet again soon.'

'I'm sure we will. Try not to be too sad. Life isn't so bad, look where we are,' she said, with her arms open to the sky.

'Merci Françoise.'

****

We were standing holding hands at the foot of the metal staircase leading up to the rear entrance of the DC-3. Janet's parents and Bruce were already inside the plane. Janet was the last passenger to have to board. John was flying the plane to Nairobi, and he had agreed that Janet could sit in the cockpit for the landing in Nairobi.

'Sweetheart, I miss you already,' I said.

'Darling, we'll write to each other, and you'll come and visit me in the UK. That should be lots of fun.'

'Yes, that'll be great. We had such a great time together these last two months. I will always remember them.'

'So will I,' as she kissed me full on the lips.

'You'd better go sweetheart. I'm going to miss you so much. You'll never know how much.'

'I'll miss you too. Heaps.'

I squeezed her hand one last time. Janet walked up the steps. She turned back as she got to the top. I blew her a kiss, as she did too. And then she was gone.

I walked away from the plane as it was getting ready to taxi off. I waved at John in the cockpit as he began to manoeuvre the plane, lining it up to roll down the landing strip. I saw Janet wave to me from one of the small windows. I waved back. I watched the plane as it picked up ground speed before seamlessly taking off and leaving Mwadui behind. It was only as I started walking away that I noticed that Françoise was there too.

'Ah, bonjour Françoise! I hadn't seen you were there.'

'Bonjour Michel. Yes, I was seeing off a friend who had stayed with us for a few days.'

'That's nice.'

'Are you okay?'

'Not really. I'm really sad to see Janet go.'

'I understand.'

'Thank you. I'm sorry I'd love to talk, but I'd better go because I don't think I'm going to be very good company for chatting. I'll see you around.' I began to walk away heading towards the Land Rover.

'Michel, wait,' as she caught up with me. 'I know this sounds odd, but do you play squash?'

'A bit, but not very well. I only just started playing. Why do you ask?'

'Well, eh, I thought that perhaps we could play a game. It could help you get over your sadness. Anyway, it's just a suggestion.'

'That's very kind of you.'

'So, would you be interested in playing, maybe later this morning? My children, Isabelle and Didier, are at school.'

'Okay, sure. What time were you thinking?'

'Let's try for 10. Hopefully, no one is playing, otherwise we'll try for another time.'

'Okay, sounds good.'

'I'll see you there then?'

'Yes, I'll be there.'

'That's great. It should be fun.'

The squash session was a disaster, at least for me. Françoise completely dominated every game. She took no prisoners and played to win. I like that approach, but only if I win.

'Well, I certainly need to lift my game,' I said, as we were walking towards the cars.

'It's your technique you have to work on Michel.'

'What am I doing wrong?'

'Your basic problem is that you need to position yourself at the top of the T so that you control the game. This forces your opponent to move around you and waste a lot of energy and time.'

'I see.'

'Now because you are young and full of energy you were able to hit the balls even though you were running around a lot. But your shots were not good because you were simply reacting to my shots, not controlling the game.'

'Thank you for those very useful tips. You need to know Françoise that I really hate losing. So, we'll need to play again soon, so I can improve my game and maybe even beat you.'

'That sounds good to me. I'm happy you've taken your loss well. You're a good sport, especially given Janet's departure. So when would you want to play again?'

'How about tomorrow, same time?'

'Okay, I see you aren't a quitter. Let's check the availability and book then,' she said.

We went back to the squash court and booked not only for the next day but the rest of the week.

'Well, I'll see you tomorrow then. Hopefully, I'll be less of a pushover,' I said with a smile. 'It could get boring for you otherwise.'

'I'm sure you'll learn quickly.'

'I intend to.'

'A demain, alors.'

'Oui, à demain. Au revoir.'

After one week of playing an hour each day, I got better. I even managed to win a game here and there. Françoise had to now work harder to keep on top. I felt better.

'You've really got better very quickly, Michel. Maybe it was a mistake on my part to give you those tips about how to improve your game.'

'It clearly was,' I said, with a cheeky smile.

'Now it's up to me to lift my game.'

'Yep, that's what it looks like,' I said, grinning from ear to ear.

'Well, I suppose I asked for it. But then I'm not too bad as an old woman playing against a young man!'

'And how old is this old woman? I asked.

'Thirty-two, and the young man?'

Seventeen in a couple of months.'

'Incidentally, you'll need to move fast to lift your game because at the end of next week, I'll be going back to Belgium,' I said.

'When next week?'

'Friday.'

'I'm really sorry to hear that it's so soon.'

'So am I. I've really been enjoying our games and your company.'

'So when will you be back in Mwadui?'

'Next summer, in June.'

'Maybe we can write to each other once in a while,' she said.

'That's a great idea. I'd like that a lot.'

'Okay, it's a deal.'

'Make sure to have the post office put interesting stamps, as I collect stamps.'

'Okay, I'll make sure.'

'So, shall we have our game then?' I asked.

'Yes, of course.'

'Your serve. You lost the last game,' I said with a big smile.

****

Sitting in the virtually empty BOAC jumbo jet to London, I thought about the incredible summer vacation I'd just spent, with Claudia visiting, the day trip to Lubumbashi, the safari, and the intimacy with Janet.

I had said farewell to Janet only two weeks ago, but I already missed her so much. But each time I thought of her the image of green-eyed Françoise appeared and would overpower Janet's.

7

Mwadui – Françoise (1973)

I couldn't believe it had been a year since I was last in the DC-3 heading towards Mwadui. But here I was again in the cockpit looking at the amazing scene rolling in front of me, with millions of galloping animals accompanying us on the way. And while I was happy to be coming back to this beauty, I was sad to think that Janet in her light-yellow summer dress wouldn't be there this time to welcome me upon my arrival. I thought of the time I went to visit her in Southampton six months earlier and how disappointing it had been. Taking the ferry from Ostend to Dover had been fun but seeing her in the UK was simply not Africa. Instead of the wide-open spaces, the warmth and the smell of the bush and the intimacy of days gone by, we were cramped in a small apartment, the weather was wet, and I saw more of Janet's brother than her. Everybody was disappointed and we also knew that it was the end of our relationship. Without Mwadui we had little or nothing to sustain the relationship. It was a very sad ending to a beautiful beginning.

'I'm going to go and sit with Mum for a while,' I said to John who was focussing on the instruments.

'Sure, Michel, we'll be another thirty-five minutes.'

'It's great to be back here with you and John,' I said to Mum as I sat down next to her in the front row.

The Green Elevator Cage

'It's fantastic to have you back. I miss you so much when you aren't with us.'

'I miss you too when I'm at boarding school a million miles away.'

'I know it's hard for you too, but there's no other choice for your education. With us moving so often and living in weird places where there is no proper respectable schooling, it was always best that you continued going to boarding school in Belgium.'

'I know. But sometimes it's difficult. And I know I have Mammy on the weekends. But it's not the same without you. It can get very lonely sometimes.'

'Oh Michel, I'm so sorry you feel like that,' she said, as she squeezed my hand. 'But look. Here we are all together again in beautiful Mwadui for the next two months. Let's all enjoy it while we can.'

'You are right. But is it definite that we'll be leaving Mwadui for good at the end of August?'

'Yes. The Tanzanian government has decided to nationalise all positions at the Diamond mine, and that includes the pilots.'

'That's so sad, especially since we only arrived less than two years ago.'

'I know, but that's the way it goes, darling. So, let's enjoy our next two months to the fullest.'

'You're right.'

'Also, the good news is that John and I will be in Brussels for the foreseeable future until he can find another job.'

'That's true. And we could have lunches again at the Rue des Bouchers as we used to in the past.'

'Of course. That would be lots of fun,' squeezing my hand again.

****

The next morning, instead of turning right as I left the driveway to go to the swimming pool, as I said to Mum I would, I turned left to go to Francoise's house. I took with me a flacon of Coco Chanel I had bought for her at the duty-free store at Heathrow. Unless her schedule had changed in the last year, I knew she would be home alone. The kids would be at school and her husband at work or out in the field looking for new diamond sources. I saw her Volkswagen Beetle Bug as I approached her house. My heart was racing. The palms of my hands were clammy. I could feel that my face was flushed.

I walked up the four steps up to the front door. The door was open, but the flyscreen door was locked.

'Hello, anyone home?' I called out from behind the flyscreen door.

Silence.

I called out again, 'Anyone home?'

'Who is there?' a voice called out from inside.

'C'est Michel.'

The sound of footsteps could be heard moving quickly towards the front door. And then I saw her. She was wearing a light green, summer dress which accentuated the greenness of her eyes.

'Quelle belle surprise!' she said, with a smile of genuine delight. She opened the flyscreen door to let me in.

I gave her the traditional European two kisses on the cheeks.

'Please come in Michel. It's so great to see you. I knew you were coming home for the holidays, but I wasn't sure when exactly. A year is too long between visits.'

'I've brought you a small gift. I hope you like it.' I gave her the perfume. I was nervous, unsure what to do next.

'Thank you so much for that,' she said, as she took the present. Her fingernails were bright red. 'Please sit down. Make yourself comfortable.'

I'd never been inside Francoise's house. It was surprisingly ordinary for someone who had sophistication written all over her. She opened the small package, and her eyes brightened up when she saw what it was.

'This is so very kind of you. You really shouldn't have done that. And I don't even have a present for you.'

'Don't worry about it. I wasn't expecting one.'

She looked at the present once more and then, most unexpectedly, she leaned down to where I was sitting and kissed me on the lips. A short but sweet kiss. Before I knew it, she was sitting cross-legged on the couch across from me. She had shapely, smooth, tanned legs, with perfectly painted bright red toenails, matching her fingernails. She was wearing flat sandals with a big toe strap, the type that is worn all over the Middle East. Her low-cut dress suggested firm breasts. She had her light brown hair up in a chignon revealing her delicate, gracious neck, just as I remembered it a year ago. The slightly salty taste of her lips was still lingering on mine. Even though it wasn't even 10 o'clock, it was already getting quite warm. The ceiling fan was on and there was a slight breeze flowing through the open window and the flyscreen door.

'It's great to see you again Françoise. I can't believe a whole year has gone by since we last saw each other.'

'I know. It's crazy.'

Silence.

'Can I offer you something to drink? A Coke? A lemonade?'

'A Coke would be great.'

'Great. Let me get you one. I might have one myself.'

While I was waiting, I could hear Billy Paul's hit "Me and Mrs Jones" which had been released a few months earlier.

'That's such a great song,' I said, as she sat down.

'I know. I love it. There's so much in it.'

'I want to tell you how nice it was to get your letters and get the news of Mwadui. I always looked forward to receiving them.'

'That's great. Letters are important to keep people together. I love letters because of the slow-motion nature of the conversation between people separated by thousands of miles. It gives time for people to think about the response they will get to their letters.'

'That's right. And because it's on paper, never to be erased, people think carefully about what they write.'

'So, how does it feel to be back?' as she took a swig of her Coke.

'Fantastic, just fantastic! I love Mwadui.'

I had a sip of my Coke.

'And how are things with you?' I asked.

'They're fine. Life does get a bit boring around here at times.'

I looked at her legs, thinking how attractive they were.

'Well, we can make things more interesting for you. We could play squash as we did last year.'

'That's a great idea,' she said.

'Have you played much in the last year?'

'Not regularly, only once in a while. I don't really have a partner to play with.'

'Well, that's more than me. There are no squash courts in Belgium. So, I suspect my game is now pretty poor.'

'So, in that case, why don't you and I play regularly? We would both improve our games.'

'That's a great idea! From what I can remember I was getting better at the game thanks to your valuable tips,' I said with a cheeky grin on my face.

'You were Michel. But we can't let that go to your head. So how about starting tomorrow morning?'

'I'm ready. Tomorrow morning it'll be. Let's say 10 o'clock.'

'That's great. I'll book the court this afternoon when I go to the pool with the kids.'

'Excellent. I'll probably see you there later then.'

****

We played squash every day, always in the morning when her kids were at school. She played very well, and initially, I had to work hard to keep up with her demanding games. But by the end of the first week, I was getting back into it. She was no longer able to dominate the centre of the court as easily anymore. I was beginning to catch her on the back foot. I looked forward to those games not so much for the challenge of the game but to simply be with her. We had lots of fun in the process of playing. Because of the heat, poor ventilation, the humidity and the running around, we sweated a lot. There was a lot of deep breathing. And our confinement in a relatively small space accentuated the feeling of intimacy between us. I could feel the sexual tension between us rising, as we played game after game in the sweltering heat of the court. The game was increasingly no longer about squash, it was now so much more than that.

At the end of a particularly hard session, as we were about to leave the squash court, I don't know what took me, but I walked over to Françoise and kissed her full on the lips. We were both completely drenched in sweat. She responded immediately, with passion and determination. Our hungry tongues continued the game, as did our marauding hands, exploring new territories, new tastes, new contours and sweet lands. We went into a frenzy of kissing, biting, licking, touching, caressing, squeezing. We had been waiting for this moment in silence; starved without admitting it, fearing the consequences, hungry to move forward. The storm had finally broken.

'We... We need to stop now Michel,' Françoise said haltingly.

'...You're right,' as we continued to fondle each other frantically.

'We can continue later... at home,' she muttered between hungry kisses, not trying very hard to stop our embrace.

'...Yes, we'd better stop,' I said reluctantly, as I opened the small access door to the court. 'I'll see you later ma très chère,' giving her a departing kiss.

I left the building, flushed, hot and sweaty, with my heart ready to jump out of my rib cage. I didn't know what to think, what to do, where to go. I decided I'd go to the swimming pool for a change of scenery after getting my swimwear from home.

'Well, hello, stranger. We haven't seen much of you since you got back,' Judy said, as I got close to the usual suspects on the grass at the swimming pool.

'I've been catching up with Mum and John.'

'I understand. So, what's new?' Judy asked. The others were half listening, half talking to each other.

'Not much really.'

Silence.

'Actually, I'm trying to absorb the fact that we'll be leaving Mwadui for good in a couple of months or so. And that's hard to take in when you know that Mwadui is really paradise on earth.'

'I'd heard that this was on the cards, but I didn't know that'd it be so soon.'

'Yes, it's happened very quickly.'

I couldn't help thinking of what had happened earlier on the squash court. My mind and heart were with Françoise not with this group of people I had lost interest in and would probably never see again after leaving Mwadui. So much had changed since last year when Janet was here.

'I'm going to get a Coke. Anybody want anything?' I asked as I was getting up.

'No, we're all good,' a couple of the guys muttered.

'Michel, before I forget, we're going to start badminton nights. Would you be interested in joining us?' Judy asked after I got back with my Coke. 'We thought we'd do it every evening at seven pm in the main sports hall. Nothing heavy. Anyone who's there can join in the fun.'

'Yes, that sounds good. Could be fun, not that I'm that great at it.'

'Who cares? It's for fun.'

'Okay, count me in.'

****

Later in the afternoon, as I walked into the swimming pool area, I could see Françoise and her two children on the far-left side of the grassy area. My heart skipped a beat. I had to make an instant decision; go and stay with the usual crowd or sit with Françoise. I veered left and walked over to Françoise in full sight of my friends who would have been wondering what was happening. But quite frankly, even though it was awkward, I didn't care what sort of rumour this would generate; I was leaving in a couple of months. My heart was beating fast.

'Bonjour ma chère,' as I got close enough for Françoise to hear me.

She turned her head around, and as soon as she saw me, smiled brightly.

'Bonjour Michel. Quelle très belle surprise!'

She was wearing the same cute knitted yellow bikini I had seen her in last year. The kids were playing in the wading pool some thirty metres away.

I put my towel down on the grass a respectable distance from hers.

'I haven't stopped thinking about you, Françoise,' I said in a whispered tone once settled down. I briefly glanced across to where my friends were sitting. They didn't seem to be paying any attention to me. That was good.

'Me too, Michel.'

'When can I see you again alone?' I asked.

'Jean-Pierre is out of town for a few days looking for diamonds or whatever he's doing in the bush. Why don't you come over this evening?'

'I'll try, but I can't promise.'

'I'll be waiting for you.'

Those words of promise fed my already hungry appetite for Françoise's most inviting body. I reached out to touch her, and she promptly responded by squeezing my hand, before quickly withdrawing it. Just as well I was lying on my stomach to hide my eagerness.

I stayed with her for a couple of hours. I read a couple of French stories for her children, Diddier and Isabelle. Françoise and I spoke about everything under the sun, mainly to distract ourselves from the main game of wanting to passionately embrace each other as soon as it would be humanly possible.

'I'd better go, Françoise. I'll see you later.'

'Okay, à bientôt J'espère.'

****

As soon as I reached Françoise at the swimming pool the next day, I could tell from the body language that she wasn't happy.

'Where were you last night? I waited for you most of the night.'

'I'm so sorry, but I simply couldn't make it. I had to join the guys at the badminton tournament last night. I had sort of promised them that I'd join them.'

'Was that really more important than coming over to my house?' she asked, with a bitter tone in her voice which hurt me to hear. I was scared of losing her even before anything had really started.

'I did say that I couldn't promise that I'd make it.'

'If you had time to go and smash a stupid little feathered object over a net, I'm sure you would have had time to visit me,' she said, with the faintest sound of pain in her voice.

'I'm so sorry I kept you waiting for nothing. Believe me. Please. I would have come over if I could have left the badminton game without drawing too much attention.'

'It's just that I was so looking forward to seeing you. And then you didn't come,' she said, with such a tone of disappointment. It crushed me.

'Oh Françoise, I'm so sorry. Really sorry. I didn't realise how much you were counting on my coming over last night.'

'Of course, I was.'

I reached out to touch her hand. Like the previous day, she responded by squeezing my hand briefly.

'I also don't want to completely cut myself off from my friends. They give me a cover that might well be useful later, which includes spending some time with them.'

Silence.

'I understand. I do,' she said, with a half-broken smile.

Isabelle was coming over with her little brother. 'Maman, viens jouer avec nous dans la piscine.'

'Of course, darling.'

Françoise got up to join her children. 'I won't be long. Don't go,' she said in a whispered tone.

'No rush. I've got a book to read.'

I stayed a couple of hours. And like the previous day, we spoke about life, politics and everything under the sun.

The Green Elevator Cage

We were comfortable with each other. We liked each other's company.

'Françoise, I promise tonight I'll come over. I will first go to the badminton game and then leave early.'

'I'll be waiting for you, Michel. Please don't disappoint me again,' reaching out to touch me. I squeezed her hand briefly.

'A bientôt, ma chère,' I said, as I left her.

****

I left the badminton game early, pretending to be tired and that I needed to go home to sleep. I drove straight to Françoise's home and parked the Land Rover at the back of her house. I didn't want to make it obvious I was there. Mwadui being a small community, everyone knew everyone's car. I was both nervous and excited in anticipation of what was going to happen next. I felt flushed. I was a ball of nerves. So much so that when I got to her front steps, I knocked over two empty milk bottles and broke them in the process. Françoise came out right away when she heard all the noise, wondering what was happening. It was a very poor beginning to what was meant to be a very special evening.

'Bonjour, Michel. Quite the entrance!' she said, with a big smile.

'I'm so sorry, Françoise. Let me quickly clean this up.'

'Don't worry, these things happen.'

After picking up as many of the glass shards as I could, relying on the poor lighting over the front door, I stepped into the house. Almost on cue, we immediately embraced and repeated the same frantic dance of our tongues and hands as we had a few days earlier on the squash court.

We were starved for more discoveries after days of deprivation. She then took my hand and led me to her bedroom, the most intimate part of her home. I was keen to discover more of Françoise's body, but I also wanted to savour this beautiful moment. I began to slowly undo the front buttons of her light, yellow summer dress. There were many of them, but as I slowly undid the buttons one by one, more of her smooth flesh was revealed, more of her breasts were exposed, her nipples came into view, her belly button showed, and finally, her white lacy undies discreetly appeared. The dress fell to the ground. She went into the bed and slid over to give me room to join her. I undressed quickly. We continued our journey of mutual discovery, but this time in a less frenzied way. She guided me, showed me what she liked, and like a flower opened herself to me.

Together in the bed, we were wrapped in boundless passion and endless desire. The air was warm, but not hot; the ceiling fan was quietly whirring above us, and a slight breeze was flowing through the open window, waving the sheer curtains into the room and caressing us as we gently undulated on this African summer night. It was a perfect moment when all the planets were lined up. And even though we knew it wouldn't last, we held onto that moment as if it would never end.

After lighting her cigarette then mine with Claudia's lighter, we lay next to each other propped up against the bed board. The moonlight was streaming in, as was the Hollies' "The Air that I Breathe" from the living room where she'd put on the LP.

'That was so beautiful, Michel.'

The Green Elevator Cage

'It was fantastic, chérie,' softly caressing her breasts, teasing her nipples and running my hand down her tummy.

'Now do you see what you missed out on by not coming over yesterday?' she asked playfully, as she leaned over to kiss me on the lips.

'Yes, and trust me, it will never happen again.'

'So, why don't we fix that mistake and play some more.'

'That's a great idea!'

I thought how beautiful life was, as I rolled over to kiss her nipple.

****

After our first evening together, we took every possible opportunity we could find to make love. And while we tried to be careful, mindful of the dangers of getting caught, many times we took big risks because our lust for each other quite simply controlled us. Our favourite getaway was the bush. Our escapades would always be around mid-morning when Didier and Isabelle were at school. We would take with us a blanket and a small picnic basket filled with fruit, biscuits, cake and wine. We would drive out of the fenced-off area in her VW Beetle Bug looking for a secluded area where we could settle down and discreetly indulge in blissful intimacy. The combination of her emerald-green eyes drawing me into her world and the sweet scent of the opened French flower in the sun-drenched African bush was quite simply paradise on earth. Nirvana lasted almost two months.

One day, however, our exploits came very close to crashing down with potentially painful consequences for all. Françoise and I were in her bedroom one morning. It would have been around eleven o'clock. She was sitting on the edge of the bed, only wearing her lacy undies, having already taken off her dress and her bra. I was standing by the bed shirtless close to her. She was about to take my shorts off when we heard a car drive up the driveway. I looked out the open window.

'What the fuck!? It's Jean-Pierre! I'm out of here.'

I grabbed my shirt and ran out of the room, down the hallway, into the kitchen and out the back door, slamming the flyscreen door behind me. I could hear a car door being closed. I never ran as fast in my life. I made a quick left to get some cover by bushes and avoid being seen in an open field. I felt I was living through a very bad, second-rate movie. My adrenalin was pumping like crazy, giving me that extra booster to get away as fast as possible from the scene. I was saved from being caught because that morning my mother needed the Land Rover, so I decided to walk over to Françoise's house.

When I got home, John was in the garage working on the car's engine. I was flustered, exhausted and out of breath, having just run for dear life.

'Are you alright?' John asked, looking up from underneath the open bonnet of the car.

'Yeah, sure... Perfectly fine... I've just been running a bit,' I said, still trying to catch my breath.

'Michel, I've been meaning to talk to you about something.' He was now standing next to the car.

'Yeah, what is it?'

'You seem to be spending a lot of time with Françoise.'

'Yeah, so? I like being with her. We have good conversations. We talk in French.'

'I'm sure but I'll get straight to the point; are you involved with her romantically?'

'What!? Are you joking? Of course not, not at all,' I said, appearing to look aggrieved.

'Really?'

'Yes, really!' I said, raising my voice and pretending to be shocked I was even being asked this question.

'The reason I ask is that sleeping with someone else's wife can get you into very deep trouble.'

'But I'm not doing anything of the sort.'

'Good, I'm happy to hear. Because there'd be nothing I could do for you if Françoise's husband came after you to beat you up. Nothing. And he would have every right to do so.'

Silence.

'You understand that. Right?' John said, looking straight into my eyes.

'Yes, of course.'

'Good.' He went back to working on his car.

I walked away and went to my bedroom. I felt flustered.

That afternoon I went to the swimming pool as I always did and to my relief, I saw that Françoise and the children were in their usual place at the far end of the grassy area. I went straight to them. My friends were as usual clustered to my right. I waved at them and continued on. They waved back.

'Are you alright, chérie?' I asked.

'I'm fine. It was a bit of a close call, but I managed to duck into the bathroom and get dressed.'

'Why had he come to the house?'

'He had apparently forgotten important papers he needed for work.'

'In any case, it was a very close shave,' I said. 'On top of that, John was home when I got there huffing and puffing. He quizzed me about our relationship, but I denied everything.'

'Good. We'll need to be more careful from now on,' discreetly reaching out to squeeze my hand.

'Yes, this town is too small to play these liaisons dangereuses,' I said, with a smile.

****

From then on, we were very careful to avoid potentially compromising situations. But we also knew that time was fast running out. Both our families were leaving Mwadui permanently on the same day. So, we didn't change our routine. We continued to go out in the bush for our illicit picnics in the mornings, and in the afternoons, we would be together at the pool with the children. We didn't want to waste any valuable time. During one of those last afternoons when we were together at the pool, the subject of my father and his failure to get in touch with me came up again.

'I don't want to shock you, but have you thought that maybe the reason he hasn't been in touch is because he actually may not be your father?'

'It's a possibility I have increasingly thought of,' I said, looking at her children playing in the wading pool in the distance.

'It would explain a lot, Michel.'

'I know. I probably don't want to hear it for some reason.'

'I understand.'

'Claudia also believes that's quite probably the case.'

'Which would explain why your mother is keeping very quiet about it all, hoping it would all go away magically!'

'What do you mean?'

'I suspect your mother is probably ashamed about the whole situation and that's why she's avoiding dealing with it,' she said, getting up to go and check on her children.

'You're right. Whenever I try to bring up the subject, she always finds an excuse not to talk about it.'

Françoise stayed with the children for a few minutes and then came back with them. She then asked Didier if he could take a picture of us and Isabelle. So, we went to lean against a fence close by, with Isabelle standing in front of us. Françoise had her arm behind my back with her hand on the small of my back. Being only six years old, Didier wasn't quite sure how to take the picture. The camera was like Claudia's, a Kodak 104. After a lot of prompting, we eventually heard the click of the picture taken, like theatre curtains coming down.

****

One morning, a few days before our departure, I went to Françoise's house. The front door was open, and the flyscreen door unlocked. I looked inside, I could see that she was lying on the couch, but she was facing the wall so she couldn't see me. I let myself in. Packing boxes, some closed, some open, were scattered everywhere. Roberta Flack's "Killing me softly with his song" was playing. Like me, she always liked to have music in the background. I walked over to the couch. Françoise had tears running down her cheeks. I knelt on the floor and took her right hand. I touched the tears with my finger and rubbed the moisture on her lower lip. I then kissed her lips. They were pleasantly salty. I did this three, or four times until her tears stopped running. She turned her head towards me, revealing her eyes filled with such sadness and pain.

'Oh, my dearest Michel, I'm so happy to see you. You're my sunshine.'

'Ma chère Françoise, why are you crying like that?'

'All this, Mwadui, you and me, happiness, fun, is going to end very soon. It's so sad.'

'I know, chérie.'

'And what will I be going back to? Cold, grey France, with a husband I hate.'

'I know. It's horrible, but you have your beautiful children, and that's a big, big plus.'

'You're right about the kids, Michel. I adore them. I could never imagine not having them close to me. But I'll no longer have you. And that saddens me so much,' squeezing my hand. 'So much.'

'Me too, chérie. A lot.'

'We've had such a beautiful time together these last two months,' she said, smiling warmly at me.

'We have. I never thought this would ever happen. It was pure bliss,' I said, as I was caressing her forearm.

'You gave me such happiness, so much joy. Every day I would so look forward to seeing your smiling face.

'Oh Françoise. Que je t'aime!'

'Let's go make love, mon amour.'

'Do you think that's a good idea after last time?'

'We'll be fine. He's gone into the bush today to do some fieldwork, but I suspect it's so he can have a last fuck with the native girls in the village.'

'You know for sure he's been doing that?' I asked, shocked by the revelation.

'I can smell it on him when he comes to bed.'

'…I see,' raising my eyebrows.

'I can't stand being close to him, let alone be in the same bed.'

'Oh ma chérie. C'est horrible!'

'And when he makes love to me, I can't wait for him to finish.'

Silence.

'And when he's done his thing, he actually says thank you, and then rolls over and quickly falls asleep.'

'But chérie, why do you even allow him to make love to you if you hate it so much?'

Silence.

'I have a sense of marital obligation.'

'Maybe I'm showing my youth here, but that's completely crazy. You must only do what you feel comfortable with, not what society says you should be doing,' I said, reaching over to give her a tender kiss on her salty lips.

'I'm seriously thinking of divorcing him when we get back to France.'

'I think you really should and reclaim your life. You are beautiful, intelligent, young and charming. You would have no problem finding a decent man, who will make you and your children happy.

Silence.

'I'm so sorry you have to live through this.'

'Merci, mon amour.'

'But you know, leaving Mwadui may be very sad, but going back to France may well be your chance to start a new life without Jean-Pierre.

'You're probably right.'

Françoise got up, took my hand and led me to the bedroom. We entered the room knowing that this would be the last time that we would make love here. A warm, caressing breeze was flowing through the open window. The ceiling fan was whirling slowly, the sheer curtains were floating in the air and the bed, unmade, was waiting for us. It was a moment full of sadness, intensity and passion. One I would never, ever forget.

****

On the eve of our departure, Bill, who was a close friend of the family, invited Mom, John and me to his place for a barbeque. He had also invited Françoise and Jean-Pierre, who was his geologist colleague. The atmosphere that evening was awkward, to say the least. I sensed John didn't particularly like Françoise and that I hadn't convinced him that I wasn't having an affair with Jean-Pierre's wife. I believed my mother suspected, but being one who hated confrontation, she wasn't going to quiz me on this issue. Françoise was nervous and not her usual, relaxed self. Jean-Pierre, an introvert, was quiet and naturally reticent. Not being comfortable speaking in English probably reinforced this trait. Did he suspect anything between Françoise and me? Who knows? But if he did, he certainly didn't show it and given what I knew about his sexual adventures in the African bush, he probably didn't care. Bill, who everyone called the rock

The Green Elevator Cage

doctor, was oblivious to the hidden undercurrents in the room.

After the barbeque, Bill suggested we play Monopoly. We all agreed that this was a great idea, probably because everyone felt down at the thought of having to leave this African paradise permanently the next day. This would get our minds off that reality.

'I can still remember playing Monopoly with Michel when he was only six,' John said, as Bill was distributing everyone's start-up cash. 'Do you remember that game?'

'How could I forget, John? That was the first day I met you and you decided to beat me at a game I thought I was very good at.'

'That was a long time ago, so let's forget about it and move on,' Mum said, not wanting any friction in what she sensed was an already difficult social situation.

'Well, John, I hate to tell you this, but I won't be as easy of a push-over this time,' I said, with a smirk on my face. 'I've learnt my lesson.'

This was a game of Monopoly I had absolutely no intention of losing, and certainly not to John. Françoise was sitting across from me at the large coffee table where we were playing. We often made reassuring eye contact, and we played footsies during the whole game. I played the game ruthlessly, taking no prisoners, except vis-à-vis Françoise. Everyone was fair game. I was pumped up and felt good. Except for a few minor setbacks, I was on a roll from the beginning, and I had luck on my side.

Starting with Jean-Pierre, who was the first to fall, I then beat my mother, Bill and then Françoise, in that order. Everyone had to then watch John and I fight it out. I knew he had no chance, having gobbled up everyone else's properties. He knew he was going down, and it felt good. I knew this was ridiculous, but this was payback time, publicly, and in front of Françoise, to boot.

'Well John, what do you think of the game? I suppose it's easier to beat a six-year-old than a seventeen-year-old,' I said, in a tongue-in-cheek tone.

'Yes, you are right Michel. For the sake of the others around the table, who are looking very bored at watching this slow train wreck, I admit defeat. Well done!'

'Thank you, Bill, for suggesting we play Monopoly. As you can see, I quite enjoyed it!' I said.

Françoise gave me a last caress of my calf with her barefoot before getting up.

The evening had gone as well as it could have, and I felt good.

****

After we got back home, and Mum and John had gone to bed, I sat down at the dinner table and wrote a letter to Françoise, one I would give to her the next day.

18 August 1973

Ma très chère Françoise,

I don't know how to start this farewell letter. It's ever so painful to write. But nevertheless, I wanted to put down on paper the feelings I have for you, what the last two months have meant for me, and what comes next.

When we started our relationship on the squash court (!), I never thought that it would become so intense and so romantic. You taught me so much, and not only sexually. With your guidance, I became a man. Thanks to you, I discovered that pleasing a woman one loves is the greatest satisfaction a man can hope for. I hope I rose to the occasion.

But you also became my best friend. Our conversations about everything and nothing were so much fun but also so meaningful. You confirmed that relationships in life are everything; they develop you and they define you. I will so much miss our intimate moments in the bush (and elsewhere) and our chats at the swimming pool. These will be moments I will always treasure and never forget.

But we always knew that the moment would come when this would all have to end. And, sadly, this moment has arrived. Not only are we all leaving Africa, but because of our personal circumstances we are having to go our separate ways. Our relationship can no longer continue. And this makes me so sad. But it is also the best for everyone. We must move forward separately.

My dearest Françoise, please don't write to me, as I won't read your letters, and I will not write to you. However painful it will be for both of us, our wonderful brief journey together must sadly stop now. My heart bleeds thinking how sad you will be when reading this. I'm in tears writing this last letter.

I will never, ever forget this beautiful African summer together. It will be part of me forever. I wish you complete happiness and fulfilment for the future; you are a beautiful person who deserves the best.

Je t'aime.

Michel.

I folded the letter and put it in an envelope. I also included a poem I had written a few days earlier. I sealed the envelope and wrote her name on the front of it. I was a total mess. Writing that letter had drained me emotionally, as I had never been before. I had just terminated a very special relationship with a woman I dearly loved. We both knew that was inevitable and the only option, but it didn't make it easier, not at all.

That night I had a nightmare; it was horrible.

Françoise and I, holding hands, are running away from Jean-Pierre, John, Mum and Bill who are chasing us. We are all on a gigantic Monopoly board the size of Manhattan. Each property is the size of a New York City block. The names of the different properties are marked on the ground in very large letters and colour-coded appropriately. We have just escaped from jail and are running along the purple properties in the direction of Fenchurch Street Station. There are many other people on the Monopoly board, but they aren't paying attention to us. The others are in hot pursuit, but we are fitter and faster than them. We can see there are hotels on Old Kent Road and Fleet Street properties and four houses on Marlborough Street. They belong to Françoise, so we are almost on safe ground. Once we get there, we rest for a minute, leaning against the wall of the green house on Marlborough Street. We are dwarfed by the house which is massive. We are huffing and puffing, but the others are closing in.

'Ça va, chérie?' I ask, trying to catch my breath.

'Oui ça va, mon amour, ça va.'

We resume running and as we get closer to Free Parking, we see there's a DC-3, engines running, waiting for us. When we get to the airplane, we run up the metal staircase in the rear and plonk ourselves in two seats next to each other. The cockpit door is open but there is no one sitting in the pilot's seat. Somehow, inexplicably, the back door gets closed, the DC-3 starts rolling, picking up speed and we are quickly airborne. We narrowly miss the top of a hotel on Whitehall, belonging to Jean-Pierre. We look out the window and we can see that our pursuers are all stuck on Free Parking.

We pick up altitude, but not fast enough I feel. We look at each other, and holding hands, we kiss.

'That was a close call, Chérie.'

'It sure was Michel, mon amour.'

We fly for a while.

'Promets-moi que jamais tu ne me quitteras,' she says, holding my hand tightly. I can see she's on the verge of crying.

'Jamais, Chérie, jamais je te quitterai. Je te le promets.' I squeeze her hand.

When we fly over the Strand, we see millions of wildebeests flowing like a massive, untamed African river, making a mess of Regent Street and spilling over the Go to Jail square.

'Isn't it beautiful, Françoise?'

'It is. So powerful, so majestic.'

The plane then makes a sharp right, dipping its right wing to turn the corner towards Piccadilly and Oxford Street. And that's when things start to go badly wrong. We had never really picked up much altitude, and that is now a big problem. Suddenly, we hear and see bullets ripping through the fuselage coming from below us. I look out of the window, and I can see natives shooting at us. More bullets are hitting the plane. And then the engine on our right side is hit several times and starts billowing black smoke. We begin to lose altitude quickly. We are over Park Lane.

'Chérie, if we can get to Go, we'll be fine and we'll be safe,' I say, knowing we wouldn't make it.

'Do you really think we'll make it, Michel?'

'I know we will, chérie,' I say, holding her hand tightly. 'Never forget that I will always love you whatever happens.'

'Moi aussi. Je t'aime tellement chéri.' Tears are now rolling down her cheeks. I can tell she knows we aren't going to make it.

We are fast losing altitude, and we have hardly made it to Mayfair. The ground is coming up to us very quickly. We are finished, the end is near, and Françoise, with fear in her eyes, knows it too.

'Kiss me goodbye forever and ever,' she says, squeezing my hand.

We kiss for eternity.

We never make it to Go.

I suddenly woke up. Startled. I was sopping wet with sweat. I then cried because I now knew I had really lost Françoise for good, for real.

****

We all boarded the DC-3 flight to Nairobi the next morning. After my nightmare, I felt a bit of trepidation boarding the plane. It was a bizarre flight, to put it mildly. As a starter, John was a passenger on the flight, and we had always known him to be the captain. Françoise was there so close but yet so far, with children she wasn't managing thanks to Jean-Pierre who was doing nothing to help. The kids kept running down the aisle towards me, calling out my name. Françoise would come and get them, and I'd whisper sweet loving words in her ear, trying not to be too obvious. It was so painful not being able to touch her, kiss her, caress her. I sat alone in the back.

Everyone went to the Norfolk Hotel, where we would all wait for our respective flights later in the afternoon. Our BOAC flight to London was scheduled to leave early in the afternoon and Françoise and her family were catching a later flight to Frankfurt on Lufthansa. In those days, the Norfolk Hotel was the only decent hotel for expatriates to go to. It was a five-star hotel, with many large comfortable lounges and beautiful gardens. It was a peaceful Eden in the middle of bustling and noisy Nairobi.

We were all milling about, settling down for a few hours of relaxation before the long flight back to Europe. No one was focused on anything specific. There was no centre of gravity, everyone had spread out into the various lounge rooms. This gave Françoise and I the opportunity to discreetly escape separately from the groups that had gathered in the different foyers of the hotel and find refuge in a part of the hotel's more remote garden. There we managed to make love very quickly and very passionately. The danger of getting caught made it so much more exciting. We also knew this would be the last time for us. We reached for eternity and instead got instant gratification. We begged for love, but we got so much sadness instead. We cried tears as we desperately kissed, licked and caressed each other. Repeatedly we avowed our love for each other, but we also knew this was the end.

No one seemed to have noticed our brief absence, probably because most people were dozing away in their own little worlds. On our return from our escapade, we sat down in one of the lounges.

'Chéri, I want to give you something that's very special to me. It's a French 1 Franc coin minted in the year of my birth, 1941. My dad gave that to me. I want you to have it.'

'That's so very kind of you. I will treasure it forever.' Looking at France's Marianne on the coin with her flowing dress reminded me of Françoise. It was a perfect gift.

'Françoise, my chérie, I wrote you a farewell letter and a poem,' I said, as my voice started to crack. 'I'm so, so sad now. I love you so. And knowing that I will never see you again is ripping me apart.' I tried to regain my composure. 'Don't open this envelope until you've taken off. It's best you be alone when you read it.'

Silence.

Clutching the envelope, and looking into my eyes, she said, 'It's best we part company here,' with tears slowly flowing down her cheeks.

'You're right. Adieu, ma très chère Françoise.'

'Adieu, Michel, mon amour.'

We touched and squeezed our hands quickly as we parted company forever. I would never see those beautiful green eyes again.

I was crushed.

On the plane to Europe, John was sitting by the window and Mum was in the middle. I said nothing, pretending to read a book, forced not to shed tears.

'You'll get over it,' my mother said to me, as she put her hand on my forearm.

'What are you talking about?' I asked disingenuously but trying to look surprised.

'Do you really think I'm blind, Michel?'

Silence.

'I've known for a long time about you and Françoise. It became obvious when I heard that you were no longer sitting with your friends at the pool but with her.'

'…I, I thought we had been discreet.'

'Sitting with a married woman and her kids is absolutely not discreet!'

'Why didn't you say something?'

'As if you would have stopped seeing her if I had.'

Silence.

'You're right. I wouldn't have.'

'You certainly didn't after John asked you about it.'

'I hated lying but I had no choice.'

'I understand but you were playing a very dangerous game young man.' She rarely reprimanded me, but the tone of her voice said it all. 'This is why it's best we're all out of Mwadui.'

'I know it was dangerous and that there was no future, but I still love her,' I said, feeling my eyes tearing up. 'I'm so sad, now. You can't know how sad I am.'

'Oh, my dear Michel, you're such a romantic. Time will heal, trust me, I know.' She kissed me on the side of my head as she wrapped her arm around me.

Silence.

'I've done stupid things in the past as well, so I can hardly be too hard on you,' removing her arm.

Silence.

'Mum, we need to talk about that past of yours. You can't keep on avoiding talking about it. I have a right to know about my father.'

'You're right. When we get back to Brussels, we'll talk.'

'Do you really promise this time?'

'I do, Michel. I do.'

Silence.

'Okay, but I'll pester you until you do.'

'I know.'

'I think I'm going to try to sleep a bit. I didn't sleep very well last night.'

'I can imagine.'

8

Brussels – The Revelation
(1973)

After finally seeing Claudia in 1969, effectively for the first time, I saw her again several times over the next four years, about twice a year. She'd come and visit and stay with me and Mammy in Brussels. After I had started at boarding school, Mum had gone back to Saudi Arabia, and later to Tanzania, where I'd go and visit during the holidays.

The last time Claudia visited us in Brussels in early September 1973, we agreed that I should come and visit her in Zurich during a school break in autumn. Mum and John were in town, the three of us having left Tanzania for good together just a couple of weeks earlier. It was great the four of us could all be together again.

As always, I accompanied Claudia to the Gare du Nord train station. It was always a sad moment to see her leave. But we had a good laugh recounting the things we had done on this last visit.

As she was about to step onto the train, holding my head between her hands and looking into my eyes, she said, 'You'll always be my little brother.'

I was puzzled. 'Why do you say that?'

'Nothing, don't worry about it.' She hugged me tenderly, went inside the train and found a seat by the window. I waved at her from the platform and blew her a kiss as the train slowly made its way out of the station. I didn't understand what this cryptic statement meant.

Later that day, I approached Mum. 'Mum, do you think we could have that chat you said we would have when we left Mwadui?'

'Sure… sure…' she said, with the merest soupçon of reluctance as one has when faced with the inevitable deadline. 'Let me get myself a drink first and I'll be right with you.'

It was a late afternoon, and the sun was flooding through the open window. We were sitting alone in the living room at Boulevard du Pantheon. She was sitting in a green armchair, and I was sitting on the couch facing her. As always, her hair was up in a chignon. As far as I can remember my mother always wore her hair up in that fashion. She was wearing a white cotton blouse and a blue skirt. For a forty-year-old, she remained very attractive and, as always, charming. Confronting her on this sensitive matter had always been very difficult for me. But I had finally managed to get her to tell me about my father.

I was very nervous. I could feel my cheeks going red. I was nervous because this was such a core issue I had been demanding my mother to give me an answer on for so long; and nervous because I was anxious about the response, I already suspected I would get. I lit a cigarette with Claudia's lighter and held it tightly, trying to get more courage from it. Finally trapped, my mother had no choice but to listen to the question I slowly but calmly asked her.

'Mum, it's been four years since I first asked you why my father hasn't been in touch with me. You said you'd get in touch with him. You haven't. I'm tired of waiting for him to come to me or for you to tell me what's happening. It doesn't take much brains to realise that there's something not quite right here. When am I going to be told the truth?'

Silence.

Even though we'd agreed to finally have this conversation, she looked nervous, uncomfortable and edgy. She took a long sip of her dry martini, carefully put down the glass on the wooden coffee table, took out one of the wooden picks with a small white onion, delicately brought it to her mouth, swallowed the onion, placed the pick next to the glass, took another sip of her drink, and then looked straight into my eyes.

'Michel, darling, I've been meaning for a long time to talk to you about this, but the moment was either never right or I wasn't in town. And now is just as good as any.'

She took another sip of her drink and put down the glass.

'Michel, I'll get straight to the point. Hans isn't your father.'

She picked up her glass again and had another long gulp. She again looked at me without saying a word, waiting for me to say something. I could tell she was very nervous. She was fidgety.

In many ways, I wasn't really surprised. And of course, the chats I had had with Claudia, especially the one in Mwadui, had increasingly solidified my suspicions. It was almost a relief to finally hear the confirmation from my mother's own mouth. It explained so much. I paused. There was a very long silence. Maybe a whole minute, maybe longer, but enough time to allow this brutal fact to slowly sink in.

'So, who's the third party, Mum?'

'He's a Swiss man by the name of Michel Maréchal. And that's why you are also called Michel.'

I needed time to take this in. There was another long silence. You could hear the traffic outside.

'Does he know I exist?'

'No, he doesn't. …well, I don't think so. A mutual friend may have told him, but I really don't think so.'

Raising my voice, quivering, 'And you waited until I was seventeen to tell me this! Why?' I could feel that I was going redder in the face. I never raised my voice with my mother.

'Our relationship was complicated. It was in the Belgian Congo, in Leopoldville. I was married to Hans, but I was deeply unhappy. I had an affair with Michel who worked with Hans. But he was engaged to get married. I didn't want to ruin his marriage plans. So, I never told him I was carrying his child.'

'That's not what I'm asking. Why did you wait so long to tell me the truth about my life? For seventeen years I was fed a pack of lies, as was Claudia.'

I lit another cigarette. My hands were shaking.

Silence.

'First, I had to wait until I was seven to be told, or rather discover by accident, that I had a sister and then 10 years later, I'm told that, oh, by the way, she's only your half-sister.'

Silence.

She said nothing. She looked at her empty glass.

'I need to make myself another martini.'

I sat there staring out of the window, waiting for her return. She came back and took another sip of her martini.

'You had plenty of chances to tell me the truth. Last year I asked you on the plane to Mwadui when Claudia was visiting us, and you hid the truth from me. Again. Why?'

'I couldn't get myself to tell you. I don't know why. I simply couldn't do it. Maybe I was worried about what you would think of me.'

'Whatever reason you gave yourself, I simply cannot believe this. It was so wrong. Simply wrong!'

'I know. You're right.'

'And Hans is just as bad not to tell Claudia.'

Silence.

'So, I suppose you never called him, as you said you would?'

'No,' as she took another sip of her martini.

'So, when were you intending to tell me and Claudia?'

'I don't know Michel. I really don't know.'

Silence.

'Of course, it all makes sense now. I knew there was something not right. Hans not getting in touch with me, ever.'

Silence.

'So how long was the affair with Michel?'

'About three months. I was so in love with him. I thought that he'd leave his fiancée, and I'd divorce Hans. And everything would be fine. But that didn't happen. I don't know what I was thinking. I was only 22.'

'When did Hans find out?'

'I told Hans when you were about a year old. It was one evening, I had just come back from a party in

Leopoldville, as I often did, and he'd stayed home looking after you and Claudia. You'd been crying a lot, Claudia was distressed, and he was very upset by the whole situation. In the heat of a big argument we had that evening, I let slip that you weren't his son. That killed our marriage. We divorced. He took Claudia and I took you. I had no choice. I was the guilty party. This was the days before the no-fault divorce.'

Silence.

'But you know Hans did something very generous which I suspect many men whose wife had cheated on them would not have done.'

'What's that?'

'Without being told to do so by the Swiss family court, he agreed to provide a monthly living allowance for you until you turned eighteen or until I remarried, whichever came first.'

'Wow, that was very kind of him.'

'I know. And I'll always be thankful for that kindness, especially after what I had done.'

'Does Claudia know all this?'

'I just told her while she was here visiting. She was very upset that I hadn't told her sooner. I told her not to say anything to you at the train station until I had spoken to you.'

'She has every right to be very upset. For seventeen years we were brought up to believe we were full siblings and now we are told that was a big, fat lie. That's so wrong. I don't understand why Hans didn't tell her either?'

'I don't know why Michel.'

'Why didn't you say this to us together when she was here instead of separately?'

Long silence. The only thing one could hear was the sound of the traffic four storeys below.

'Are you okay, Michel?'

'Not really. I need time to take all this in.' I lit another cigarette and inhaled deeply. I looked out of the window. Thinking out loud, I said, 'Now it makes sense what she was trying to tell me at the train station.'

'What was that?'

'Claudia telling me that I'd always be her little brother.'

'Of course, you will.' She paused for a while, looking out of the window as well, probably thinking of those days some eighteen years earlier. She took another long swig of her drink. 'If you want to, we can try to look for Michel.'

My response was immediate. 'I'm not interested Mum. He's not my father. He's a mere sperm donor. No more, no less. Also, what sort of guy was he? Cheating on his wife-to-be, knowing he wasn't going to leave her for you. He just wanted to have one last fling before settling down to married life. Not a man with too many principles.'

'That's a bit hard Michel.'

'Really? How so?'

'He loved me. He said so. I loved him.'

'It cost him nothing to say he loved you.' I paused. 'Well, I suppose that makes me a bastard.'

'Oh Michel, don't talk like that. I'd prefer to think of you as a love child.'

'Yeah, I suppose that does sound more respectable in good company,' I said, with sarcasm dripping off my remark.

I lit another cigarette. I inhaled three or four times in quick succession in total silence. I kept looking out of the window. The sun had shifted. Mum was no longer in the sun's path. I looked at her. Our eyes crossed.

I put my half-smoked cigarette in the groove of the ashtray, got up and left the room.

****

As expected, even though I had told her in Mwadui not to write, a letter from Françoise arrived within ten days of our return from Tanzania. I recognised the handwriting, and the French stamp affixed to it. Without hesitating, I went to the bathroom with the letter. I kissed the letter slowly and said 'Je t'aime Françoise. I am so, so sorry.' Without opening the envelope, I took the stamp off by ripping the area around the stamp, including bits of the letter inside, leaving an empty squarish wound in the upper right of the envelope. I put the stamp in my pocket. Then, without opening the envelope, I ripped it in half, then again in half, and once more in half. I dropped the many little pieces of paper into the toilet bowl, raining down like snowflakes onto a lake. I let the flakes settle on the water. I could see some bits of her handwriting, amputated from other parts of the written body, now meaningless squiggles on paper bleeding and sinking without trace. I pressed the toilet handle and flushed the whole paper mess, watching the end of the relationship go down the gurgler slowly at first and quickly picking up speed to eventually go down with a powerful sucking sound. It was a brutal and painful way to end a beautiful relationship. I felt physically sick ripping the unopened, unread letter. It was a total betrayal of Françoise. But I had no choice for the sake of self-preservation. I left the bathroom.

****

Soon after the confirmation that my sister's father was indeed not my father, I decided I no longer wanted to be known as Michel. In my eyes, it identified me with a man with few principles, if any. I wanted a clean break from all that mess. But officially changing my first name seemed too difficult and a long process. It had been complicated enough when my mother decided at the time of her divorce to change her name and my name to her maiden name, Van den Berghe. I should have realised that her changing my family name to her maiden name, and significantly her former husband agreeing to it, meant that I was not his biological son. I must admit I hadn't given it much thought, believing that she must have done it simply because it would make things easier for her to deal with official administrative matters. In any case, I decided that a good compromise would be to simply combine the first letter of my three first names, Michel, Albert and Xavier, and from now on to call myself Max. This Max would be unique, not the shorthand for Maximillian but a new made-up name, a combo of three. I was also pleased that Max was a name that was not language specific. Whether in French, English, German, Dutch or any other language for that matter, it was pronounced the same way. And because it was a short crisp name people would remember it easily.

9

Brussels – The Home Movie (2000)

The next day they sat in Juliette's hotel room to watch the VHS tape. Max had hooked up a rented VCR to the back of the television and they had decided to make this viewing a bit of an event, so they ordered a bottle of white wine. They were all very excited, but Max was particularly keen to watch this special home movie. After all, it wasn't every day that one could discover what one's biological father looked like, especially some forty years after conception.

Max and Juliette sat on the sofa and Claudia was in a large armchair next to them. They dimmed the lights. Max turned on the VCR. The film went straight into the subject matter. The setting was a swimming pool with a grassy area around it. There were two African waiters in the background, standing by an outdoor bar. There were three adults sitting on a large picnic blanket, with food and wine in the middle. Juliette, wearing a red bikini, was sitting leaning back with her arms on the blanket. Close by her side was 11-month-old Michel, sleeping. Four-year-old Claudia was next to him, caressing his head. To Juliette's right was a handsome, tall, dark-haired man, wearing bathing shorts, sitting upright with his legs crossed. At an angle to them, sitting with her legs together, was another woman in a one-piece blue bathing suit. They seemed to be enjoying themselves, laughing and waving at the camera.

Juliette, Claudia and Max were staring at the silent film intensely, not saying a word. Max hadn't known what to expect but given his fair-skin complexion and blue eyes, he didn't think his biological father would look almost Spanish. But who knows with genes, they can act very strangely, he thought. He hit the pause button on the remote.

'Okay, before we go any further Mum, we need some commentary from you,' Max said.

'What do you want me to say?' she said, with the merest hint of annoyance, discomfort and hesitation in her voice. She took a sip from her wine.

Max knew that she hated to talk about the past or anything else that made her feel uncomfortable.

'Presumably, that's Michel next to you?' Max asked.

'Yes.'

'And I suppose it's Hans who's filming.'

'Yes, I think so. It must be. It's so long ago.'

'How does it feel to see this again after all these years?'

'Very strange. It's as if I'm peeping into someone else's private life.'

'Mum, can you remember how you felt being there with your husband as well as with the father of your son and his now wife Suzanna?' Claudia asked.

Silence.

They all took sips from their wine glasses.

'I'm sorry. I can't remember. It's too difficult. It's so long ago,' she said, making a movement of the hand as if trying to shoo away the question into oblivion.

Silence.

'I just know that I still loved your dad, but I simply was not ready to settle down. I was young. I needed to live. I was twenty-three.'

'Okay, let's continue watching,' Max said, pressing the play button on the monitor.

The film continued with Claudia kissing Max's head and then getting up to go to her mum and kissing her on the cheek. Juliette held her tight, kissing her back and both waved at the camera. Claudia broke away and ran towards the camera. The film ended abruptly. It resumed but this time Hans had traded places with Juliette. Hans was kissing and playing with Max, who kept on trying to crawl away. At one point, Max slipped out of Hans's grasp, but Michel caught him. Everyone seemed to be having a good time. They all waved at the camera. Again, Claudia came running to the camera.

The three were watching in silence, mesmerized by this special home movie.

As Max watched this film, he wondered what his mum must have been thinking while she was filming the scene, perhaps something along the lines, 'I wonder how long it will be before Hans discovers the truth?' Or 'When should I tell him the truth?'

The film ended abruptly.

'Well, there it is. What a find!' Max said.

'I know. Incredible!' Claudia echoed.

Juliette was quiet.

'Are you Okay, Mum?' Max asked.

'Yes, I'm fine. I'm just trying to take in memories of forty years ago. It's a lot.'

'I know,' Claudia said.

Silence.

Max filled everyone's glass.

'Mum, this will be my last question because I know you feel uncomfortable talking about all this, but it's after all our past.' He took a sip from his wine. 'Can you remember, what went through your mind when you found out that you were pregnant but not from Hans?'

Silence.

'I wasn't actually upset because I really thought that Michel wouldn't marry Suzanna, and we would be together after I divorced Hans.'

'Had Michel promised you this?' Claudia asked.

'No, not at all. But I was so madly in love with him; I was certain that's what was going to happen.'

'You must have been heartbroken when none of that happened?' Max asked.

'I was. It quickly became clear that he had no intention of leaving his then-fiancée, Suzanna. So, I didn't tell him that I was carrying his child. I didn't want to complicate things even more.'

'It was very kind of you not to tell him,' Max said.

'I don't know. But I also know I was no saint. I had just cheated on my husband. I felt so bad because he so loved me. And this is what I gave him in return.' She took another sip from her wine. 'So, when I finally told him that you weren't his son, he was utterly shattered in disbelief. His world had come crashing down from out of the blue. I can still see the saddest expression on his face. As if, "How could you do this to me?" It was so, so sad. I begged for his forgiveness, to please give me a second chance. I was on my knees, crying, holding onto him. I was so desperate. It was the most horrible moment in my life. We were both in tears, both shattered for different reasons. I knew then that it was all over for good. I had completely messed up things.'

Max and Claudia had been listening in silence to their mother. Max could feel the total distress she must have been going through on that fateful day.

'One last thing, Claudia. You need to know that to this day I feel so bad for the way I treated your father. He didn't deserve it. Not at all.'

'Oh, Mum. Let's leave all this behind. We've said enough about all this,' Claudia said, having risen to hug her mother.

'I agree, let's go and have dinner and a change of scenery. We've had a gruelling two days,' Max said.

'Thank you. I do love you both so much.'

10

Canberra – The Renunciation Papers (2001)

In March 1997, about six months after coming back from his trip to Belgium for Mammy's funeral, Max got a letter from his mother. In it, Juliette said that she had recently received a letter from her ex-husband, Hans. Not having heard from him in well over three decades, she admitted that she had been rather shocked to receive it. In any case, in his letter, he indicated that he had recently turned seventy-two and was not in the best of health. Accordingly, he wanted to make sure that all his personal matters were in order in case he was to pass away suddenly. Juliette couldn't help herself from making a comment in the letter that this was typical Swiss behaviour. As a matter of fact, Max thought it was quite sensible. Had Mammy organised a will before her death, they wouldn't have had that ugly fracas over Bonpa's medals.

As part of his process of ensuring that there were no loose ends that other people would have to deal with after his demise, he requested Juliette to ask Max to sign an official document in which he would relinquish any rights to his estate after his death. Initially, Max was offended by this request because it suggested that Hans believed that he was the sort of individual who would seek to get a share of the estate of a man he didn't know at all. To claim such a share of the loot would be pretty much as amoral as it gets. Even in the case of an offspring's legitimate right to the estate of a dead parent, Max always thought that the benefactors acted as if it was their inherent right to a share of the estate, that they deserved it when in reality they probably didn't at all. John used to refer to it as blood money, and he had a point, Max thought. Of course, Hans didn't know him at all, except for what Claudia would have told her father about him. So Max thought that perhaps he could be forgiven.

The letter from the Swiss embassy arrived about a month later, inviting Max to come to the embassy and sign the papers. How strange life could be Max thought as he walked over to the Swiss embassy the next morning. Here he was in Australia about to relinquish over forty years after his birth all rights to the estate of a man, whose name was on his Belgian Congolese birth certificate, purportedly meant to be his father but whom he had never met; at least not since the age of one, and probably never would, given that he was not his biological father. He had no reason to. This whole situation confirmed the age-old adage that one shouldn't believe half the things one reads. Max often thought that he was a fraud, having acquired the very difficult-to-obtain Swiss citizenship simply because his mother happened to be married to a Swiss man when she decided to have a love child. But then, he thought, his biological father was Swiss after all so he shouldn't feel too much of a fake. The good news was that as a result of all those illicit dalliances in the heart of Africa over forty years ago, Max's daughter, Genevieve, also had Swiss citizenship. How funny how the world turns, he thought.

During the signing of the legal documents under the courteous but watchful eye of one of the Swiss diplomats,

The Green Elevator Cage

Max thought that this act would once and for all terminate all his ties, however strange they may have been, with Hans Sigrist, Claudia's father and his mother's former husband. Oddly, and for no obvious reason, Max walked out of the embassy feeling relieved. This loose end had finally been dealt with once and for all.

11

Jeddah – The Wall (1966-1969)

As soon as the cabin doors of the Boeing 707 were opened, the intense, humid heat came gushing into the aisle and hit them like the sudden opening of an oven door. It was intense, it made them breathless.

'Well, Michel,' here we are in Saudi Arabia!' my mother said, as she squeezed my hand. Looking out of the window, she added, 'This is really not a place where I thought I'd ever live.'

I was sitting in the middle seat between John and Mum. I was anxious, really worried. My tummy was feeling weak. I'd have to once again go to a new school, make new friends, and live in a country which until only a few weeks ago I didn't even know existed. I thought of Mammy, Uncle Pierre, our walks on Saturdays, and the butcher and the cold cuts he'd always give me. It was all so far away.

'Don't worry honey. We'll make this our home. It'll all be fine,' John said, reaching over to touch Mum's forearm.

'Sure darling, sure,' Mum said without conviction, as she looked out of the window again.

The very large sign, "Welcome to Jeddah International Airport" over the main building was clearly visible from where we were sitting, as was the barren landscape beyond the airport. As we walked down the iron steps they had rolled to the plane, I noticed, as had everyone else, that the "L" of "International" had almost fallen off and was precariously hanging there like a thumb and an index finger pointing downwards.

The arrival hall was enormous, virtually empty, and hot, with several ceiling fans whirring away uselessly high above the ground. Three large pictures of men, all wearing the traditional headdress, the keffiyeh, were hanging unusually high over the main entrance where immigration officials were sitting behind desks. Lines were forming haphazardly in front of the desks.

'Mum, why are all the men wearing white and the women are completely covered in black?' I asked as I had never seen such a sight.

'It's a custom here Michel.'

'It's strange.'

'There'll be a lot of things here that will be very different from what you're used to.'

'Whiskey, Playboy?' asked the customs man as he went through our suitcases, wide open for the whole world to see. I could see Mum's silky underwear which the customs man seemed to like touching repeatedly.

'No whiskey, no Playboy,' said John. I could hear from his voice that he wasn't pleased with the situation. The customs man was spending most of his time going through Mum's suitcase, ignoring the others. Now he was touching her bras, enjoying the soft touch of the delicate lace. He looked up at her with a satisfied grin as he was fondling the bras. Mum touched John's arm to restrain him. She could sense that things could quickly go badly wrong.

'Okay, you can go,' the customs man said, sounding disappointed, as he marked all three suitcases with a white chalk. 'Welcome to the Kingdom of Saudi Arabia. Enjoy your stay.'

We put our suitcases on a trolley and rolled it outside. We went through the main exit doors and there was Jeddah, my new home for the next three years. It was very hot.

****

Like most expats, we lived in a compound for foreigners. Ours was officially called "The Royalty Gardens". I'm not quite sure why it was called that, given that there was nothing royal looking about them and there were no gardens in the neighbourhood. The "Royalty Gardens" consisted of two rows of four grey bunker-type two-storey houses. They reminded me of the German bunkers built by the Third Reich, strewn on the Belgian beaches in anticipation of an Allied landing. I used to love playing in them as a kid. Now I got to live in one. Each identical house had a flat roof, like all houses in Jeddah, which was more like a veranda on top of the house. From there one could scan the horizon and see how flat and desolate the city was. The underdeveloped nature of the city, especially after living in Brussels and Beirut, was striking. From the rooftop, I could easily see the seven other houses of the "Royalty Gardens", or what we called "The Block". Each house was surrounded by a thick, three-metre-high wall and a large metal gate. If one stood in the middle of the front courtyard, one's horizon was about five metres. It was strange to start with, but one quickly got used to it, as with most unusual things in Jeddah.

All the occupants of the eight "Royalty Gardens" houses were families which were professionally connected with Saudi Arabian Airlines, a TWA-managed airline. All the families were American, and all the children went to the same school, the American School of Jeddah, which everyone referred to as ASJ. Given how intertwined were our lives, in the three years that I lived there, for better or worse, I got to know my neighbours very well. Our house was on one of the corners, adjacent to a large empty lot where a homeless family of three Pakistanis lived in makeshift housing constructed out of cardboard.

Of the seven other houses on the Block, four became important to me. Two houses down from us lived my friend Bob and his brother Jim. Bob and I would spend a lot of time together exchanging stamps or going to the souk to buy more stamps. Bob played the guitar beautifully.

Next door to them lived two girls, Lucy who was older than me and Georgette who was slightly younger. Like Mum, their mother was Belgian. So, we got to practise our French, especially when we didn't want anyone else to know what we were talking about. They were lots of fun to be around.

Next to them on the other corner lived the Watts. John Watts was also a pilot. They had a son, Sam, who was in my grade. He was also the bane of my life in Jeddah. He was a tall, athletic sort of guy whom the girls liked, and he always played to the gallery. He thoroughly enjoyed picking on me whenever he could. However, he did have one serious flaw; he was a lousy student who always had bad grades in all subjects. He also liked to get attention and that often got him into trouble, big trouble. He had a charming twin sister with the cutest chin dimple, April, who hated him, his lies and his constant bragging. She and

I would often study together at my house. As opposed to her brother, she was an excellent student.

Next door to the Watts lived Helen Sawyers, who happened to be my English teacher, and her husband, David, who was head of security for the airline company. Helen was one of the most beautiful and sweet women I'd ever met. I thought I was so lucky to have her as my English teacher. She was also the teacher accompanying the students on the yellow school bus as it went around the various American compounds picking up and dropping off the pupils. She had a daughter, Jill, slightly younger than me who had her mother's stunning looks. We spent a lot of time together.

Ironically, rather than being a divider between the eight families, the thick wall around each house brought us together against the outside world. We were like a little American oasis in a Saudi desert, a small fortress against strange external forces. And at the intersection of the Sawyers, the Watts, the Belgian girls' and Bob and Jim's house the kids would meet every evening either before dinner or just after on the top of the wall. We would sit on the wall and share notes on the day's events. We were like periscopes going above the water to see what was out there. We would always sit on the same two walls facing the Sawyers' house. And from our three-metre vantage point, we could easily look beyond the Royalty Gardens into the Jeddah night. It was our safe place. We called it "The Wall".

****

From my bedroom window, I could see that Bob, who was picking at his guitar, and Jill were at The Wall and that

Lucy and Georgette were making their way to it as well, climbing up the ladder they had rigged up and which was leaning against the corner of their back wall.

'I'm going to The Wall, Mum,' I said, as I was walking through the kitchen on my way to the back door.

'Okay, Michel. We'll be eating in about 20 minutes,' Mum said, without looking back from whatever she was cooking on the stove.

I climbed up the ladder I had put together soon after arriving in Jeddah and walked along the wall to meet up with the others. The wall being thick meant that walking along it took no effort and was relatively safe. No one had ever fallen off it.

'Hi guys,' I said, as I approached and sat down next to Jill, who had only had to climb up her ladder to get to the centre of the action.

'Hi Michel. How are things?' Bob asked as he strummed his guitar gently.

'Pretty good. Did you hear Sam got the paddle today?'

'Really?' asked Lucy, who had joined the group.

'What had he done this time to get it?' asked Georgette.

'He'd given Mrs Sawyers lip after she'd told him off for not handing in his homework which was due three days ago,' I said.

'Is this why he's not here tonight?' asked Georgette.

'Probably, it's pretty humiliating to get the paddle,' said Bob.

'It must also hurt,' piped up Lucy.

"Who gave it?' asked Jill.

'The principal,' I said. 'And you could hear the ten hits all the way down the corridor. It must have hurt.'

'But isn't this his third time in three months?' asked Lucy.

'I think you're right,' I said. 'And each time the paddle was given by Mr Brown.'

Then I heard my mum call my name out to come home for dinner.

'Well. I'd better go guys. See you tomorrow.'

****

I knew I was going to be checkmated in about three moves. There was absolutely no way for me to get out of this situation. Paul was quite simply better than me at chess.

'It looks like you're going to win again, Paul.'

'Michel, if you'd rocked your king early in the game, you wouldn't be in the mess you're in now.'

'I know. You're right.'

Three moves later, I was dead, once again.

'Shall we play another game?' I asked, 'before I have to get back home.'

'Sure. And you start.'

Paul was my best friend. He was the first student I'd met when I first arrived in Jeddah about a year earlier. I sat next to him in English class, and we became best friends ever since. He was slight and spoke softly. He had few friends, if any. He pretty much kept to himself. But for some reason, he and I got along well. It tickled him that I was born in Africa. It was simply unfortunate that he lived some way from my house. It took me about 15 minutes on my bicycle to get to his place. So, this meant I had to ride through an empty, desolate, dry, open space, with nondescript bushes, in what I called "No Man's Land", often pursued by packs of flea and tick-infested wild dogs. And as I was uncomfortable around dogs at the best of times, this ride to Paul's was not one that I looked forward to. Actually, it really scared me a lot. But sometimes he'd come over to my place to give me a break from the dreadful ride over to his place.

'You're very quiet today, Paul. Everything okay?' I asked as I made my opening move by moving my right rook four spaces.

Silence.

'Not really.' He moved his king's pawn forward one space.

'What's wrong?'

Silence.

'It's the usual. When I came home with my report card yesterday, Dad belted me again. But this time really hard. He screamed at me like I'd never heard anyone scream. And now my back and butt really hurt. Wearing a T-shirt even hurts. My report card wasn't even that bad. It was just an excuse to get stuck into me.'

'I'm so sorry Paul. I simply couldn't imagine John doing that to me.'

'I'll show you,' as he lifted his T-shirt. His back was covered with large, fresh welts. It was painful to look at. I could see scars from previous lashings.

I knew that his father had a very short fuse and would get very angry, very quickly. Even Paul's mother looked subdued.

'My mother is also on the receiving end of his crazy rages. It's so scary to be in the house when this happens,' Paul said, his voice full of despair.

Silence.

I moved my left rook four spaces.

'I can't take much more of this beating. If I have another bad report card, I'm going to jump off the roof rather than put up with another beating. It's so horrible.'

'Paul, you can't think like that! Please! I beg you.'

'Michel, you must promise me not to tell anyone what I told you. If my father finds out I told you, I think he would kill me. I really believe that.'

'I promise Paul. I really do.'

'Good. Let's just play chess and not talk about it anymore.'

Not surprisingly, he won the next game as well. At least there was something positive in his life.

****

A few months after starting at ASJ, I had to give a book report presentation to the class. I dreaded the day. But inevitably it was going to arrive. My tummy had been churning for the last week simply at the thought of having to stand in front of the whole class. My English was poor, and I spoke with a thick Belgian accent. Mum had helped me with the preparation, but I had this nagging feeling she didn't really know what was expected of me. And I was right.

Presentation day arrived.

'Michel, please come to the front of the class for your book presentation,' Mrs Sawyers said.

I walked over to the front of the class clutching my book and my written report.

It was an utter disaster.

I did a book review of a French comic book, not a real book for grownups. What was I thinking? I should have known better, but my mother never thought it was strange. I was repeatedly laughed at in class during my presentation. It was a humiliating affair; one I will never forget, especially since it had taken me a lot of work to put the presentation together. Mrs Sawyers was very nice about it. I managed to avoid crying. I was determined not to give any of the kids the satisfaction of seeing tears. When I was finished, I went back to my seat utterly crushed. Paul, who was sitting next to me, patted my back to comfort me.

'You'll be fine, buddy. Don't worry about it.'

'Thank you, Paul. Thank you.'

****

I knew the usual get-together on The Wall would be difficult that evening, but I also knew that I had to go to it because if I didn't go it'd look as if I was avoiding the issue, the inevitable feedback on my failed presentation.

Most of the kids were already sitting in their usual places.

I sat next to Jill. I always felt stronger next to her.

It didn't take long before Sam launched into his usual attack against me, but this time he had rich material to draw from.

'Quite a good laugh you gave us in English today, buddy,' he said, with utter contempt and glee in his voice.

Jill squeezed my hand in such a way that no one else could see it.

'You're pretty quiet, buddy. You can't talk anymore?' Sam said, smelling my humiliation.

'Could you just lay off, Sam,' said April, Sam's sister.

I said nothing. I kept my head down looking into the Sawyers' poorly tended garden below. I was hoping that this whole conversation would end soon. But it didn't. Sam was keen to milk this for all he could. We then all heard in the far distance the call to prayer from the mosque. Everybody went quiet for a while, but not for long.

'Lost your tongue buddy?' Sam insisted.

'Come on Sam, let it go,' Bob said.

Ignoring the last plea, Sam continued. 'Your only friend, Paul, had to rescue you. And he's a nigger.'

'Don't call him that!' I shouted.

'Why not? Isn't that what he is?'

There was nothing I could do. Not only was Sam bigger than me but he was sitting a long way from me on the other wall.

'Sam, back off,' said April, 'if you don't, I'll tell Mum.'

'Wow, that really scares me, Sis!'

Silence.

'So, what do you have to say about your nigger friend?' Sam asked.

'That's really enough Sam,' Bob said.

'He's my friend and I like him. He's nice to me. Not like you.'

Jill squeezed my hand. I squeezed hers back. I was shaking.

Silence.

I was rescued by Mum calling my name out, indicating dinner was ready.

****

The Green Elevator Cage

Living in Jeddah in the mid-1960s as a Westerner was a strange experience in so many ways. To all intents and purposes, we were almost totally isolated from our local environment. It was particularly hard on the mothers who were stuck at home alone all day, not allowed to drive, while the husbands were at work and the kids were at school. Their only interactions with the Saudis were with the 'houseboy', and he was generally a Yemeni. And taking a taxi as a woman alone was not an option. So, to compensate for this strange existence the eight families at "The Block" regularly held parties, mostly to forget where they were living. Although there was no formal roster as to which family would be hosting the next party, it more or less went clockwise, and they were held generally every two weeks. The core guests were the couples living at the Royalty Gardens, but other expats were also welcome to join in. Of course, having these 'cocktail parties' behind closed doors and in a country where alcohol is illegal gave it all a surreal sense. But prohibition à la Saudi didn't stop the expats from producing moonshine gin, known locally as 'Sadiki', Arabic for "friend". It was very bland and tasteless, but it was alcohol. It did the job.

It was at those parties that I discovered Jazz, as well as other adult life issues.

As children were not allowed to those parties, as a 12-year-old, I would sit on the top landing, out of sight, and listen to John and Mum having parties in the living room. I could hear the jazz slither its way up the stairs. Oscar Peterson, Miles Davis, Chet Baker, Stan Getz and so many others would be playing in the background. Frank Sinatra was another great of the period. His songs, "Strangers in the Night" and "Summer Wind" were often played.

Jobim's "The Girl from Ipanema" came out in 1964 and was often heard, as was Fats Domino's "Blueberry Hill". The music notes were intermingled with cigarette smoke and the sound of voices and laughter undulating up to my level. I would often fall asleep, and Mum would gently wake me up a couple of hours later and walk me back to bed.

At one of those parties, as I was listening to the music while sitting on the landing, Mrs Sawyers furtively came up the stairs followed by Captain John Watts. They were surprised to see me.

'Well, hello Michel, what are you doing here?' asked Mrs Sawyers.

Before I could answer, she said, 'I need to have a private conversation with John, so I thought we'd have it up here. We'll just go into your spare room.'

'Sure Mrs Sawyers, you know where it is.'

'Of course, thank you, Michel.'

They went into the room which was behind me and closed the door, and I went back to listening to Miles's trumpet notes whiffing up the stairwell. But a few minutes later, I heard sounds, moaning sort of sounds like the ones I often heard coming from Mum and John's bedroom at night, coming from the spare room. I thought it was strange. This went on for a few minutes, as Chet Baker was now playing "I fall in love too easily". After about ten minutes or so, Mrs Sawyers and Captain Watts came out of the spare room. They both looked a bit ruffled and confused. She certainly didn't look her usual neat and proper self, like I would see her in English class. She must have noticed my slight surprise.

'Michel, dearest, this will be our little secret just between us, okay?' as she pressed her right index finger on my lips.

'Of course, Mrs Sawyers.'

'That's a good boy. Well, I'll see you in class on Monday then.'

'Yes, Mrs Sawyers.'

And back down they went, as she quickly patted down her top and ran her hand through her hair. She then glanced back at me and winked at me, something I would have never expected from Mrs Sawyers.

****

At the end of my English class, after I had seen Mrs Sawyers and John Watts at our party, Mrs Sawyers asked me to come up to her desk.

'Michel, I have been thinking, and I think you could do with a bit of help with your English class. So, I thought I could give you private lessons after school. And then you could come back home with me on the bus. What do you think?'

'I think that would be great. Thank you so much. I'd better check with my parents that it's okay.'

'I'm sure they would be fine with it. Tell them I'll do them for free.'

My parents of course approved of the lessons. But they were a bit surprised as to why Mrs Sawyers agreed to give them for free.

'I wonder why she's doing this. That's very generous,' my mother said, as we were sitting at the dinner table.

'I don't know why, Mum.'

I loved the private lessons with Mrs Sawyers. I was so lucky. The lessons allowed me to be with a most beautiful woman. This was indeed really a special treat. The only thing was that I had to put up with the teasing from the kids about getting those lessons. And Sam was the leader of the nuisance pack. The lessons went on for several months. And the encounters on the steps during parties happened each time my parents held a party.

****

Soon after arriving in Jeddah, I discovered the wonders of the souk; a maze of narrow lanes full of activity where the sun struggled to get through, of shopkeepers selling every imaginable thing, of sounds of voices buzzing and objects rattling, of older men huddled together smoking hubbly bubblies, of lots of people milling about looking for a good bargain, and where colourful cloth, gold and foreign currencies from faraway lands were equally available. It was truly an amazing place, especially for a 12-year-old. This is where I met an old, bearded man who sold stamps in a small shop, which was literally not much more than a hole in the wall. His name was Mohammed. I immediately loved that man's peacefulness and the serenity he projected. And even though I only knew a few words of Arabic and he only knew a few words of English, that, combined with hand signs, enabled us to communicate and 'discuss' stamps. I always looked forward to seeing him. I'd probably go and see Mohammed once a month or so during the three years I was in Jeddah. I'd stay with him while John and Mum shopped around elsewhere. I can still see him, sitting cross-legged on a rug at the front of his shop. He would always give me a broad smile whenever I came to see him. We had a ritual hello 'system'.

I'd say, 'As-salaam 'alaykum.'
And he'd respond by saying, 'Wa-alaykum-Salaam.'
'Kayf halak?' I'd ask.
'Zayn, Al Hamdu Lillah,' he'd respond.

He'd order tea for the two of us and we'd both sit on the rug, drinking very sweet tea from small cups. And then we'd look at stamps for an hour or so. I simply treasured those special moments with Mohammed. Using up all my pocket money, I bought many stamps from that wonderful man over the years.

On one of my first visits, I discovered an old French stamp I had been looking for, for a very long time and one I needed to complete a specific series. He saw how my eyes brightened up when I saw that missing stamp. The stamp was in a small transparent envelope to protect it. He let me hold it. There it was, the valuable, missing French stamp, in a Saudi souk, of all places. But it was too expensive for me to be able to buy it. I'd have to save my pocket money for the next two years to be able to afford it. Nevertheless, each time I went to visit him, I'd ask to see the stamp. And he would kindly oblige. And after looking at it very closely, I would give it back to him.

'Shukraan,' I'd say.
And he would reply, 'afwan', placing his hand on his heart.

****

20 May 1967

Dear Claudia,

How are you? I hope you are well.

I'm sorry I haven't written to you sooner. I often think of you and wonder how you are going. I really hope that we'll finally be able to meet one day. I think it's very strange that I have a sister I've never met. I can't wait for the day!

Jeddah is a very strange place. Arab men wear white and their wives, usually three or four of them, follow him three steps behind all dressed in black! They would be very hot underneath all that cloth. They also look like penguins, except that the penguins are probably cooler.

When I go out with Mum and John, we often go to the souk which is where we do our shopping, but not for food. I've met an old man who sells stamps. His name is Mohammed. He's so wonderful. He looks a bit like Santa Claus, with a long white beard. He has beautiful stamps in his shop, even a French one I've been looking for so long. I wish I could buy it. We spend a lot of time together even if I can only say a few words in Arabic.

The streets here in Jeddah are nothing like the ones in Brussels. When I go out with my bicycle I get chased by wild dogs. I get so scared, but I have to continue. Maybe that way I'll get over the fear of dogs. Did you know that there's no real garbage collection here? People just throw out their garbage on the street and then the different animals (dogs, cats, camels, goats, buffalos) come and eat the scraps. It really smells awful on hot days which is often in the summer. But what is really bad and sad is to see poor people picking at the garbage hoping to find food they can eat or bring back home. There's one man I often see at the garbage heap. He lives in a vacant lot next to our house on the other side of our very high walls, so we don't see him. His home is made up of cardboard boxes, many of which we threw over the wall because Mum knew he could probably use them. Because I saw him several times, I started talking to him. I found out that he's from Pakistan and he lives with his young wife and a small baby. He invited me over to his home one day. It was so sad to see how they lived. They have almost nothing. The little baby sleeps in a wooden crate, and they sleep next to him on cardboard. It's difficult to speak with him because his English is not very good. He and his wife work for a very rich Saudi prince who has a mansion on the other side of the street. He told me that he gives them leftover food but will not allow them to stay overnight on his large property. He explained to me because he wasn't an Arab, they had to live the way they did. But he was thankful to God he had a job.

My best friend is a black boy. He's from Georgia in America. He doesn't believe I was born in Africa because he thinks my skin should be black. So silly! There are some nice kids on the block I live on. There are even two girls from Belgium. So, I can speak in French with them and no one understands what we say. That's fun. I have another friend, Bob, who also likes to collect stamps like me. We exchange stamps all the time. He plays the guitar. And there is Jill, who is a beautiful girl I like a lot.

I'd better go. I wish you could come and visit us. I could show you all the strange places and people. It would be so much fun.

Lots of big kisses and hugs.

Michel

P.S. I lost a tooth (molar) in class yesterday and it was very embarrassing. Lots of kids made fun of me.

✷✷✷✷

One day, when tensions in the Middle East were very high, just before the outbreak of the 1967 Arab Israeli War, Sam had the stupid idea of drawing a big Star of David on the blackboard and writing in big print underneath it: "WILL WIN OVER ARABS". The principal Bob Brown happened to walk by the classroom and saw what Sam had written on the blackboard. Brown was known to lose his temper easily, but I had never seen him so angry as that day. He came storming in. He looked even bigger than he already was.

'Who is the idiot who wrote this on the blackboard?' he shouted, pointing to the blackboard behind him.

He was fuming. His face had gone completely red. A vein on his forehead had swelled up most unnaturally. We all looked down. No one said anything.

Silence.

'The longer the one who did this takes to come forward, the harder I will be on this student. Much harder.'

Silence.

'Okay, this is the deal. I'm going to go back to my office. I'll let you discuss this among yourselves for twenty minutes. If the one who did it doesn't come to my office by then, I will expel all of you from school for three days and this will go on your official records. It's your choice.' He stormed out.

All hell then broke loose. Everyone turned on Sam, like starving hyenas on a fresh carcass.

'I'm not going to be expelled because of your stupidity Sam,' one of the students shouted at Sam. 'Same here, Sam. You are a fuckwit and I'm not paying for your behaviour,' said another. 'You're a shit, Sam, and you'd better go and admit to the principal otherwise my dad will make sure to tell him you did it,' said another. Several others echoed the same sentiments. Absolutely no one backed Sam. He was alone and he knew it.

'Okay, Okay, I get the picture,' Sam said, raising his hands in defeat, as he walked out of the classroom and headed down the hallway towards the principal's office to face the firing squad.

We all went back to our desks and waited in silence, anticipating the inevitable sound of the paddle coming down hard on Sam's posterior. And, indeed, it wasn't long before the familiar sound of wood hitting flesh came rushing down the corridor. We all counted the hits in silence. The sentence had been doubled to twenty hits. In a somewhat sadistic way, we waited for him to see his face but to our disappointment he didn't come back to class that day, having been sent home for the rest of the day.

Luckily for Sam, this episode was quickly forgotten because the next day the principal decided for safety reasons to close the school for the rest of the term. As we were close to the summer school holidays anyway, it didn't make much difference. We all thought it was very exciting to be involved in this war, which, of course, we weren't.

The closest the war came to us was on the radio. For the next six days, the duration of that short but decisive war, Mum, John and I would be huddled around our Panasonic Zenith radio listening to the news. The BBC was reliable, but the Saudi national radio was not so, given that they made up their news stories as they went, stating outlandish things that were utterly divorced from reality. A typical assertion would be something along these lines: 'Our sister Arab nations have shot down 25 Israeli planes in several encounters, but, sadly, we lost one.' Not surprisingly, listening to the radio became a source of entertainment for the expat community.

As we had no television and no telephone, the radio played an important part in family life for us and all our friends. It was our lifeline to the outside world. We heard all the big events on the radio, the assassinations of Martin Luther King and Robert Kennedy, the riots in France, Nixon's election, President De Gaulle's resignation. But the most memorable one was without any doubt the first man landing on the moon on 21 July 1969. John and Mum organised a cocktail party for the occasion. Any excuse would do for one, not that they necessarily needed one. By the time we heard Neil Armstrong's famous words crackling over the radio as he set foot on the lunar soil, 'That's one small step for a man, one giant leap for mankind', most of the guests were half intoxicated with sadiki and didn't care if Armstrong had landed on Jupiter. The party continued as if nothing had happened, with Chet Baker blowing his horn and Duke Ellington hitting the ivories. Things could be surreal in the oasis.

However, even in Jeddah, we couldn't completely get away from the war in Vietnam. Sometime in mid-1968 my mother and I went visiting a family friend in one of the other compounds. The latest issue of Life Magazine happened to be on the friend's coffee table. I picked it up and began to leaf through it. Then something caught my attention. This issue had the mug shots of all the GIs who had died that week in Vietnam. There were many of them, several pages. Three hundred and twelve GIs, according to the article.

'Look Mum, most of these soldiers are black, like my friend Paul.'

She looked across and turned a couple of the pages. 'It's very sad Michel. So many mothers must be desperately missing their sons now,' she said, as she took my hand and held it tight. 'I would never want to lose you, certainly not like that.'

I brought up the subject at the dinner table that evening.

'John, today I saw in Life Magazine all these pictures of the GIs who've died in Vietnam in just one week. There were hundreds of them. It was so awful, so sad.'

'War is an ugly thing son. But sometimes it's necessary to lose one's son to protect the country's freedom.' He was noisily munching away on the iceberg lettuce on a small side plate to the right of his main plate.

'Really?' I asked, surprised.

'Yes, really. What would have happened, if we hadn't sent our sons to stop Hitler?'

Silence.

'Would you expect me to go to Vietnam?'

'Yes, I would.'

'But I could get killed.'

Silence, except for John crunching on his iceberg lettuce.

'This conversation is completely ridiculous,' Mum said, visibly upset. 'Michel isn't even American. And in any case, why would you want to see Michel die in a stupid war that has nothing to do with America?'

'That's what patriots do, honey.'

'Oh really? Don't tell me about patriots! My father fought during WWII for four years, first in the Resistance and then in the British Army with Montgomery in North Africa. He came back changed, damaged and aged. He was not the father I had known before the war. And I really believe he died at fifty-one because of the war. I'll never allow my son to go through that stupidity and die for someone else's war.'

Mum was shaking. She was holding tightly her napkin, bringing it to her eyes to dry her tears of anger. I had never, ever heard her raise her voice with John.

Silence.

John got up, threw his napkin on the table, and as he walked away, he said, 'No son of mine will be a draft dodger.'

Mum sat there across from me, weeping silent tears which were rolling down her cheeks. I was so sad for her.

'Ça va, Mamam?' I asked, as I stretched my hand across the table to comfort her.

'Oui, tout va bien Michel. Tout va bien, chéri,' as she squeezed my hand.

****

The Green Elevator Cage

Soon after the draft dodging episode something horrible happened to Paul. I will never forget it. Never.

We'd arranged that Paul would come and see me one Saturday afternoon. He was always punctual. And if he was late, even by just a few minutes, he would apologise profusely. When twenty minutes had already gone by since he was meant to have arrived, I really got worried.

'Mum, Paul should have been here a long time ago. I think I should go and see what's the problem.'

'Give him a few more minutes. I'm sure there's a good reason for him being late.'

I could sense something was wrong. He'd never been late in the two years we'd been friends. Never.

'Mum, he's half an hour late,' I said, in desperation. 'I need to go to his house and see what's the problem.'

'Okay, Michel, but be careful. You know that I always worry about you going alone to Paul's. Do you want to ask Bob to go with you?'

'No, I'll be fine.'

As soon as I got out of the compound, I jumped on my bike and rushed in the direction of Paul's house. I pedalled like crazy, hoping that by doing so everything would be okay. Halfway through "No Man's Land", I saw his inert body next to a bush in the distance. I pedalled even faster to get there. And then I saw him, his face down in the dirt. There was blood everywhere. On his face, his body, his buttocks. His shirt was ripped, and his pants had been pulled down to his knees. He was moaning, reaching out with his hand for help. I could see the scars on his back from his father's beatings. I cried. I threw up. I kept crying for all his pain, now and before. I held his hand. I didn't know what to do as a thirteen-year-old. It was too much.

'Paul, I'm here,' I said, trying to comfort him. 'What happened?'

'I'm in pain, real pain. Please get help,' he moaned.

'Okay, I will Paul. I promise.'

I knew there was a teacher who lived not far, on the edge of "No Man's Land". I jumped on my bike and rushed to his house. Luckily, he was home, and he opened the door. After quickly explaining the situation as best as I could between tears and cries, we jumped in his car and easily got to Paul. We got him into the car and sped to his house to let his family know. Paul's mother screamed in despair when she saw Paul. Together we brought him to the hospital. We were all in shock and silent. Together we held hands in the hallway, worrying about Paul and even more about Paul's father's reaction to the attack.

I went to see Paul at home a couple of days after he was discharged from hospital. He was sitting on his bed. Not doing anything, simply staring at the wall.

'Are you Okay, Paul?'

'Not really.'

'I'm so sorry about what happened to you.'

Silence.

'What did your dad say?'

Silence.

'He said I should have put up a fight, not simply give in.'

'But you told me there were three grown men. You were outnumbered!'

'I told him that, but he just said that was no excuse.'

Silence.

'He showed no warmth.' And then Paul started to cry. 'He didn't even hug me. Nothing. It's as if he didn't want to be close to me.'

Paul kept crying.

His loneliness, his sadness was tearing me apart. I didn't know what to do, or what I could do to help my friend.

'You'd better leave Michel; I need to rest a bit. I'm on these painkillers and they are making me very sleepy. I'm really happy you came over because I know how much you hate going through "No Man's Land", especially now.

✦✦✦✦

I came back a few days later. He was sitting on his bed, looking at a comic book.

'How are you today?'

"I'm a bit better.'

'Do you want to play a game of chess?'

'Sure, why not?'

As Paul was taking one of my bishops he said, 'My parents and I have decided it would be best that I go to a military academy in Georgia in the new school year in September.'

'Wow! That's a big decision. Are you happy with that?'

'It was actually mine,' as he took the other bishop and progressively broke through my poor defences.

'I understand why you're doing that. You've always been interested in going to a military academy.'

'That's right. And anyway, I was going to go to one next year.'

'But you're my best friend. It'll be very lonely without you.'

'I know, Michel. And you are my best friend too, but it was inevitable that we would eventually have to go our separate ways. I simply cannot go back to ASJ.'

'I know. I understand.'

'Anyway, the good thing about going to the academy now is that I'll avoid my dad's regular beatings. I can't take it anymore.'

'You're right.'

'But I'll miss my mum and sister,' he said, as he moved one of his rooks to avoid a pawn's move against it.

I moved my queen forward by seven squares. I had to somehow counter his usual effective offensives.

'There's a good academy in Georgia close to where my grandparents live, so I'll be able to see them regularly. And if I stick it out with the academy, I can more easily join the Marines after high school.'

'You really want to do that, don't you?'

'Yes, I do. Hopefully, they'll be less racist in the Marines. And they'll pay for my education.'

'You sure have it all sorted out. I don't know what I want to do later. The only thing I know is that I'll go to boarding school in Belgium next year.'

'Michel, I hate to tell you this, but you're going to lose again,' he said, almost apologetically.

'One day, I will win. I simply have to.'

'Well, you'd better hurry up because you're running out of time,' he said, with a smile on his face.

****

I knew the meeting at The Wall wasn't going to be easy that evening, but I couldn't continue avoiding it.

The Green Elevator Cage

I could see, as I was walking along the wall that there weren't many kids, many of them having gone back to the US during the summer holidays. The two Belgian girls were there, as were April and Sam, Jill and Bob picking at his guitar. Luckily there was a spot available next to Jill.

'Eh, long time no see buddy. Where have you been?' asked Sam, in his usual mocking tone.

'Just doing things.'

'Really now?!'

'Yes, really. Helping John out with work he's doing on the patio.'

'Rumour has it that your nigger friend was cornholed last week. Is that true?

Bob stopped playing the guitar and looked across to Sam.

Silence.

'Well, so what's the story?' Sam insisted. 'Was he, or wasn't he?'

Jill, who was sitting next to me, put her hand on top of mine which was resting on the wall. Sam saw Jill's comforting move.

'Oh, now you need a girl to give you support.'

'Why do you always have to pick on Michel? Please leave him alone Sam,' April said.

'And yet another girl to help you out. What a wimp you are,' Sam said, with utter contempt in his voice.

I was so angry with Sam, but I knew there was little I could do to defend Paul. 'Paul will always, always be a much better person than you. You are a bully and always will be. I'm going home.' I got up and started walking along the wall.

'Yeah, run away to mummy.'

As I walked away, I could hear Sam ask, 'Anyone care to join me for a joint?'

****

One evening at dinner time, my mother told John, 'I heard from the girls on The Block that David Sawyers broke into John Watts' house when they were out and burned cigar holes in all his suits and jackets.'

'Really?! Why would he do that?'

'Don't you know that John had been fooling around with Helen for quite a while?'

'No, I didn't know. Well, then I suppose he deserves it,' John said, as he kept eating his meal.

'John would be very upset because we know how much he loves his clothes.'

'That's all going to complicate things when we have our next party,' John said.

A few days after I had found out about what had happened to Captain Watts's suits, I was coming into the class after school had finished, looking forward as I always did to the private lesson with Mrs Sawyers. She was sitting at the desk, as always, but she seemed different. Somewhat stiff-looking. Before I could get to her desk, she said, not in her usual warm voice but in a cold, matter-of-fact tone, 'We won't be having a lesson today, Michel, nor in the future.'

'Why Mrs Sawyers?' not able to hide my disappointment.

'Michel, things have happened in my personal life and as a result, circumstances have changed. I will no longer be teaching.'

Silence.

The Green Elevator Cage

'I will miss your classes and our after-school lessons, Mrs Sawyers.'

'I will miss them too, Michel. But you have really improved a lot since you first arrived at ASJ. So, I don't think you need those after-school lessons in any case.'

'Thank you, Mrs Sawyers. It's thanks to your lessons that I got so much better.'

'You're a smart young man. Work hard and you'll go far.'

'Thank you so much, Mrs Sawyers. Can I come over later and see Jill?'

'Michel, I think it might be a better idea to come another day next week, maybe.'

'Okay, Mrs Sawyers. Please tell her I'll miss not seeing her.'

'I'll tell her. You go now.'

****

The next morning, I sat next to Jill on the school bus. She was already on the bus, as she got on at the first stop. It was always great to start the day seeing her.

'How's it going Jill?' I asked as I squeezed her hand.

'I'm fine, but things are really bad at home. My mum is having an affair with Captain Watts.'

I thought of all those times Mrs Sawyers and Captain Watts would come up during the parties and make strange noises behind the closed door of the spare room.

Feigning surprise, I asked, 'Are you okay?'

'Not really. How could she do this to us? I feel so betrayed.'

Having known for two years, what could I possibly say to comfort her, I thought.

'My dad is really, really mad. I'm not sure if he's madder with my mum or with John for burning holes in his suits. I think John.'

'I can imagine.'

'My dad is like a dog with a bone. I know that he really wants to get John for that.'

Silence.

'Does your dad know that Sam smokes weed?' I asked Jill in a low voice.

'Why do you ask?'

'Well… with his contacts with the Saudi police, he could let them know, somehow.'

'But if he did that the whole Watts family would be kicked out of the country in like forty-eight hours.'

'I know,' I smiled. It would take care of two problems, John and Sam, I thought selfishly.

Silence.

'You could casually tell your dad in a conversation.'

'I can't do that!'

'Why not? Your dad hates John, and Sam would be missed by no one.'

We were fast approaching the school.

'Think about it.'

The bus had stopped, and everyone was getting off the bus.

'I've got to run. I'll see you later,' I said.

✳✳✳✳

Three days later word quickly went around that the Watts family had forty-eight hours to leave the country. I could hardly believe that, soon, I would no longer have to put up with Sam's nastiness. I would, however, miss April.

She'd helped me a lot with schoolwork over the last three years. I owed her so much. And she had such a cute chin dimple. But given the most unusual circumstances of the Watts's sudden departure and the utter chaos that would be permeating the household, sadly it would be impossible for me to drop in to say farewell to April. I'm sure she'd understand. As for a farewell party for the Watts, that certainly wasn't going to happen given the bad blood between two of the families on The Block. Instead, they effectively left in the dead of the night, as if they had never existed.

****

The inevitable time was fast approaching when I would have to leave Jeddah to go to boarding school in Belgium. The Saudi authorities didn't allow ASJ to have classes beyond 7th grade because they didn't want all these Western teenagers roaming around Jeddah. All my fellow students from the 7th grade cohort were going back to the US. The only logical place for me to go was back to Belgium, the closest thing we had to "home" base.

'But Mum the last time I lived in Belgium was when I was eight, and now I'm thirteen.'

'I know it won't be easy to start with, but don't worry you'll be fine. You've done very well with all the changes before.'

'I finally got to live with you and now I have to leave you again and go to boarding school.'

'I know, Michel. But you'll get to see Mammy every weekend, and I bet you she'll cook you rabbit often the way you like it.'

'It's not the same as living at home with you.'

'You'll visit us during the holidays, and I'll write to you every week.'

'And also, it's going to be a French-speaking school. I haven't been to one since Beirut. I probably don't know a thing about all the complicated French grammar.'

'Michel, stop worrying. If there are problems, I'll organise private tutoring for you.'

I wasn't convinced by any of Mum's arguments, but I also knew that I had no choice. I'd have to go. I could only hope that boarding school wouldn't be too horrible.

****

When I knew that I was going to leave Jeddah, I went to see Mohammed the stamp man to give him the bad news that I would no longer be seeing him, that we would no longer have our hour-long conversations. I was very sad because I always looked forward to seeing my old friend and drinking tea with him.

Using my hands for rudimentary sign language, I put my right hand on my heart then made it flat and made it go up in the air like an airplane. And then made a sad face and pointed alternately to each of us. I made it clear we would no longer be meeting. He looked sad as well.

Silence.

We drank our usual tea from the little cups.

He then went to his special cache of valuable stamps which was a small, locked box. He unlocked it with a small key he had in his pocket, opened it and took out the old French stamp I had been eyeing for three years. Holding the stamp in his right hand, he put it to his heart and then gave it to me.

'Haditi lak.'

The Green Elevator Cage

I simply couldn't believe it. 'Shukraan jazilaan lak,' I said.

I delicately took the stamp and then spontaneously kissed the back of his old, wrinkled right hand, with veins like worms burrowing their way under the skin. I had tears running down my cheeks. I got up with a very heavy heart. I walked away slowly, and as I was about to turn the corner, I waved to him one more time and he put his right hand to his heart and then waved back. I knew I would never see him again. But the memory of his warmth and generosity has always stayed with me, certainly each time I see a French stamp. I am richer for having known him.

****

On the last evening, before I had to leave Jeddah for good, I went to The Wall after dinner. It was later than usual. I can still vividly remember that evening because there was a full moon, so bright and so near that you could almost touch it. It was a full house. Everyone was already there, waiting for me. As usual, I sat next to Jill. We held hands. Bob was strumming his guitar. And then he began to play my favourite song, "The House of the Rising Sun". We all listened in silence.

'We have a small present for you, Michel, so you won't forget us once you've left Jeddah,' Jill said, as she handed over a small package wrapped in yellow paper. I carefully and slowly unwrapped it to avoid ripping the wrapping. And there it was, a packet of 100 stamps from the Middle East. They knew I particularly liked stamps from the region.

'That's so nice of you to do that. I'll never forget this.'

'You probably already have many of them, but you can always exchange them when you are at boarding school,' Jill said.

'We bought them from your friend Mohammed,' Bob said. 'We told him it was for you. So, he put in a few more of his own.'

There was a separate envelope which I opened and in it, I saw that there were a few French stamps, including a very difficult one to find.

'Thank you so, so much. This means heaps.'

'We'll miss you, but maybe we can see each other when we visit Belgium,' said Georgette.

'That would be really nice.'

I felt so sad all of a sudden at the thought that this was indeed the last time we would all meet on The Wall, our special safe meeting place for the last three years. And with Sam no longer there, all tension was gone, and the atmosphere was relaxed. I looked up and the moon had moved. Bob was humming a tune.

'Well, I'd better go guys. It's getting late and I have an early start tomorrow.'

After teary goodbyes, I walked off towards my house. Jill followed me. We went down the ladder into my back garden. We walked around the house and stopped around the corner, away from any prying eyes. We had gone there a number of times in the last year. We kissed awkwardly, as thirteen-year-olds do. It was simple, clumsy, not sophisticated. But we were close, and we also knew this was it. Life would move on.

'You can touch my breasts if you want to. That's my farewell present, Michel.'

I didn't need to be told twice.

But then I heard my Mum call out from the back door, 'Michel, time to come home. It's late.'

'Quick, and then you'd better run before you get into trouble.'

So, I quickly ran my fingers up her T-shirt and felt her training bra. I pulled it up so that I could touch her small, perky breasts. They felt so soft, tender and delicate. I was in heaven, kissing Jill. I wanted to remember this moment forever.

'You'd better go now, Michel. Really.'

We kissed one last time and squeezed our hands. She went up the ladder and I went to the backdoor. We waved to each other and blew each other kisses. I would never see her again, and still today, after all those years, I wonder whatever became of her.

****

'Are you alright, Michel?' Mum asked as we were sitting in the plane waiting to take off. John was not with us, not having been able to take the time off.

The Boeing 707 was slowly filling up. Most of the passengers were expats, probably going back home, to a place closer to their hearts.

'Yes, I'm fine. I'm just sad to leave behind all my friends I'll probably never see again.'

'I know. It's hard. But you can write to each other and keep in touch.' She squeezed my hand.

'It's not the same. And then on top of that, I'm having to go to a French-speaking boarding school.'

'Try not to think about all that. Just think, soon we'll see Mammy. She'll be so happy to see you again. She loves you so much.'

'I know. I'm really so happy that we'll see her soon. It's been too long.'

I looked out of the window, and I could see the airport terminal. I also noticed that they had repaired the "I" of "International". It was now pointing upwards. It was a good sign.

12

Canberra – Collège de la Salle (2003)

It was a beautiful, sunny Sunday morning in early February. Max was opening his birthday presents in the living room. He loved this room, with its spotted eucalyptus polished floor and large floor-to-ceiling windows on three sides. As it was on the first floor of the house, it had the feeling of being in a tree house. The house was surrounded by a gorgeous native garden with a wide variety of different wattles, callistemons and other Australian plants which attracted all sorts of birds, turning the place into a large, open-air aviary but where the birds were free to come and go.

'Open this one first, Papa,' four-year-old Genevieve said, pointing to a small package with her index finger. 'You'll like it a lot.'

'I'm sure I will. Okay, I will then.'

'Forty-two. Wow! Where has the time gone?' Jane said.

'That's an excellent question I ask myself more and more,' Max said, as he was ripping the wrapping paper off the little box.

'Come on Papa, go faster,' Genevieve said.

'Okay, chérie. I'm sorry I was a bit too slow for you!' Max said, giving her a kiss on the forehead.

'No guessing what's in it,' Jane said, with a cheeky grin.

'Let me guess. A Jazz CD, maybe?' Max responded, opening the little red box to find a pair of silver cufflinks, with a rivulet of gold running through them. 'Wow, these are beautiful, darling!' He got up to give Jane a peck on the lips and a big kiss on Genevieve's cheek. 'I think I now have as many cufflinks as the number of years I've lived on this planet.'

'Yes, your collection is getting pretty serious. You must be the only academic who wears cufflinks.'

'I can tell you that most academics wouldn't even know what cufflinks look like, let alone own any.'

'You must fit right in with all your Marxist mates in the department, darling.'

'Yes, absolutely, even the ones who aren't Marxist. But then, as you know, I wouldn't care what they think.'

'I know. That's what I've always liked about you. You're so independent-minded; none of this group-think stuff.'

'I suppose the problem with that is that it hasn't made me many friends. Well, I'm used to that.'

'Papa, why don't you open your other presents?' Genevieve said, getting bored with the conversation.

'Okay, j'ouvre chérie!'

'Je t'aime, Papa,' Genevieve said, as she reached over to kiss him on the cheek.

'Je t'aime aussi, énormément.'

For the next half hour, they had fun opening the other presents. Janet made some more coffee, and he read her a Tintin comic book from one of the many he had kept from his childhood. He'd spoken to her in French since she was born and, as a result, she was fluent in it. He was always impressed with a child's developing brain which never confused two languages. By the time he had read about half the book, she was asleep, as she usually was when he read to her. He picked her up and brought her to her bedroom and lay her down on her bed next to her many soft toys.

'We have such a beautiful child, darling, thanks to you,' he said to Jane as he sat next to her on the couch. She had put on a Mozart quintet CD.

'We did it together, sweetheart.'

'I know, but you know what I mean.'

'Of course, I do. You know I'm so happy that Genevieve is bilingual thanks to you. It's such a great asset.'

'I know. It really is.

'So, are you happy with your prezzies?'

'I am. I really like the cufflinks.'

'I liked them too, as soon as I spotted them at the Roberts Art Gallery in Civic.'

Silence. They listened to Mozart for a few minutes.

'You know turning forty-two makes me think of Beirut and the awful time I had there.'

'Remind me again of what was the issue with that place?'

'Well to start with, forty-two was the number that was given to me by my teacher at the French-speaking, Catholic College de la Salle school in Beirut. I was nine years old.'

'Why that number?'

'Because I was the forty-second pupil to join that class towards the middle of the year, I think. Because there were so many kids in the class, the teacher found it easier to identify us by a number rather than by our names. Not very personal really,' Max said with a sardonic grin.

'That's a lot of kids in one class!'

'That's for sure. We were three to a wooden bench. Pretty crowded really.'

'I can imagine that you didn't fit in very well.'

'That's the understatement of the year, darling!'

'So, what was it like?'

'If you have a few minutes to spare I can give you an idea of what it was like.'

'Of course, I have the time. And anyway, it's your day so it's your call what we do.'

'Why don't you get us a glass of wine each and then I can entertain you.'

'Okay. I always like to hear your exotic stories. Always interesting.'

While Jane was in the kitchen, Max quickly went downstairs to check how Genevieve was doing. As expected, she was sound asleep. He covered her up and gave her a kiss on the forehead.

He can still remember on the rare occasions his mother would stay overnight with him and Mammy in Brussels; she would kiss him good night in the same way.

Jane came back with two glasses of wine and sat next to him on the couch.

'Okay, here's a glimpse of my days in Beirut in 1965.' Max took a sip of his wine.

Jane took a sip of hers and settled back.

'My teacher had thinning hair which he greased and combed back. One of his teeth, his left canine if I remember correctly, was made of gold. He had a very round face that made him look like a cartoon character. I remember him calling me to his desk at the front of the class on the first day. I was the only non-Lebanese pupil, so I must have intrigued him. As he was talking to me, I noticed how well manicured were his fingernails. But what really struck me were the nails on his pinkies, they were both very long and curved. They were like talons, the sort you'd see on a rooster. It's only later that I found out why he let these grow. He used them to regularly explore the inside of his nose and ears.'

'Nice touch!'

'Yes, really. But it gets better.'

'He was also a very nasty and sadistic man who enjoyed beating the students with a horse crop he always carried around with him, like a marshal with his baton. He'd call the students to the blackboard by their assigned number, usually four or five at the time. This would give him the opportunity to use with great pleasure his horse crop on the pupils. And when he did, he would lash out with all his might like a madman. He'd hold the child's left arm around his armpit with his left hand and strike the child with the crop in his right hand. To avoid the lash, the child would inevitably move forward, and the teacher would too. So, the two would end up going in circles, with the child screaming in pain and the teacher shouting at him to stand still. It was horrible to watch. All the kids would shout for him to stop, which he only did after getting tired of the exercise. This usually happened twice a day.'

'That's so ghastly!'

'But I was lucky that he never hit me. I think. I'll tell you why. On the first day, John had my mother tell him in no uncertain terms that not only did he not believe in corporal punishment but if he ever put a hand on me, he would break every bone in his body. I can still remember that conversation very well because my mother didn't quite use the same frank language in her translation. But it was clear that the teacher had got the message loud and clear. He also looked at John's physique and he quickly realised that he was no match for the man who did forty push-ups every morning and had been a PE teacher in the US Army.'

'That's funny,' Jane said, as she took a sip from her wine.

'It was in a way. A bit like a bad movie,' taking a sip of his wine. 'But while in a way this was good news, in another it was bad news as well. Already, I was the odd kid out, not being Lebanese and not speaking Arabic, but not being lashed by the teacher meant that I was being seen as getting special treatment. This was another reason why I had absolutely no friends. No one wanted to be associated with me in the playground during lunchtime. I really couldn't win. Those were very lonely days. So, you can understand why each time I hear or see the number forty-two I think of that creep of a teacher.'

'I sure can darling,' Jane said, holding his hand.

'Sadly, I was stuck with that school. Because John refused to give any baksheesh to get his pilot's license with one of the local Lebanese airlines, we were in a very tight financial situation. And so, there was no way for me to go to an international school.'

'Sometimes I wonder about your mum and John and how they brought you up.'

'Me too!'

Max took a sip of his wine.

Thankfully, we were in Beirut for only seven months or so. But there were fun times too. We lived in two different hotels: the *Strand* and the *Normandie Hotel*. I particularly liked the second one because it was, I think, family-owned and smaller. You can imagine how, as a nine-year-old, I loved running around throughout the hotel, exploring every nook and cranny. The staff loved me. I read a while ago that the bar of the *Normandie Hotel* was where British MI6 agent Kim Philby, who had been a notorious and ruthless Soviet spy for decades, would meet his Russian controller. We missed each other by a couple of years!'

'That's incredible!'

'I know. But my most memorable times were when John and my mother's many pilot friends and their wives would get together to drink and party in the very same family-friendly, smoke-filled *Normandie Hotel* bar. Music by Frank Sinatra and Dean Martin would be playing in the background. These were friends they had known since the days of the Congo. They were like family. I had met them many times in Brussels before. It was my introduction to the world of 'non-skeds', the freelancers of the aviation business. Those are days I'll never forget.' Max took a sip of his wine.

'How boring was my life living here in Canberra compared to yours in all these exotic lands.'

'Sure, but there was a price to pay. Little stability, a real sense of not belonging anywhere, always being an outsider, uncertainty, fear of the future, different schools; some weird, few friends, really too much change for a child.'

'Still, look what a fascinating person this has turned you into, Max!'

'Okay, I have one last story from the Beirut days and then that's it. I don't want to bore you.'

'Not at all, darling. You've got such great stories to tell.'

'On our last day in Beirut, John sold our Volkswagen to a close pilot friend at the airport while we were waiting to board our flight to Jeddah. For some odd reason, I remember his name well, Sam Swabsky. He paid John cash in US dollars, carefully counting each bank note. I can still see it because I had never seen so much real money, not Monopoly money, as a nine-year-old. Only in the movies. He was a Telly Savalas-type-looking guy. Putting his big arm around my shoulder, he said, 'Your parents are bringing you to a strange place. So be careful in Saudi Arabia. It's an odd place where men hold hands in public, but men and women are not allowed to do so. Men wear white and women wear black. That's not normal my boy. Be careful.' I never forgot those words of caution. And you know what, he was spot on. But little did I know it at the time.'

'You know Max, I'm often amazed that you turned out half normal,' she said with a big cheeky smile.

'You're very funny, darling! I love your sense of humour.' They gave each other a spontaneous peck on the lips.

They each had a sip of their wine.

13

Florida – Boca Raton (2010)

'You certainly haven't lost your touch in making dry martinis.'

'Thanks, Mum. Years of practice as you know. I can still remember making them in the Congo when I was 15.'

They were sitting by the swimming pool of the house on the waterfront that she and John had bought in Boca Raton, Florida, a few years back. John wasn't there, having gone to California for a few days to visit one of his sick brothers. The afternoon was coming to an end slowly, along with the dimming light. A slight, warm breeze was caressing them as they sat there listening to the local jazz station playing American standards.

'Yes, that's a few years ago. Those were fun days, with all the pilots coming to our house to drink all our booze but never bringing any themselves. Bunch of freeloaders,' she said.

She took a sip of her drink and then delicately took one of the toothpicks out with a small cocktail onion at the end of it. She put it to her red lips and slowly slid it off the toothpick. Max would have seen her do this ten thousand times over the years.

'I wonder whatever happened to the tall pilot. You know the one with a large moustache. He must've been at least six foot seven,' Max said.

'Yes, I remember him well. Bill Dobson. You used to run towards him and ask him what he wanted to drink. It was always the same answer, 'Scotch on the rocks, but easy on the rocks, boy.' He'd drink three bottles for each one he brought.'

'Yes, I remember those days as if it was yesterday. He lived in Kisangani with his very large family. I think he had eight or nine children. I went there once with John by DC-4. It took several hours to get there from Kinshasa. What a boring trip! The only thing there was to see was the canopy of the jungle below.'

'I can well imagine that you would have been bored.'

'Especially that this was during my precious summer holidays from boarding school when I came to visit you in the Congo.'

Max took a sip of his gin and tonic. 'Still, his house was fun. We went to it while we waited for the plane to be fuelled up for the return flight. They had a baboon living in the house. He'd jump on the back of the armchair and check if you had any lice or other tasty, little bugs in your hair. It tickled how this baboon would check out your scalp, looking through your hair. I'll never forget that.'

Silence.

'So do you know what's happened to him?'

'I think he died because he drank way too much.'

'Do you know where he died?'

'I think somewhere in Southeast Asia, but I'm not sure.'

'I'm not surprised. What about the other characters? Do you know what's happened to them?'

'Tom Delaney died in a plane crash in the Congo somewhere in the jungle some years back. We never found the plane, let alone his body. He was probably flying one of those poorly serviced planes that no one else would fly. So sad.'

'That's horrible.'

She took another sip of her drink. 'I think Joe McWilliam is now in Windhoek in Namibia where he's started a company. I believe a few of the guys have joined him there,' she said.

'Apropos of nothing, when it rains hard in Brisbane, I automatically think of Africa and the sweet smell that comes just after the rains. I always loved seeing those massive clouds on the horizon and that sense of knowing that a serious downpour would soon be coming.'

'I know. It was always a great feeling. And it was like clockwork, always at the same time every day.'

The evening was fast settling in now. Except for the light coming from the living room, they were almost in the dark.

'Would you like another drink, Mum?'

'Will you have another one?'

'Yeah.'

'In that case, I'll have one too.'

Max got up and went to the bar.

As he was walking back with the drinks and a small bowl of olives, she asked him, 'So, how are you liking Australia? It's been almost thirty years now, right?'

'Yeah, thirty years. I love it there. It's home.'

'That's great, darling. Who would have thought you'd ever settle there.'

'I know. I love the country, the people, the attitude; basically, the whole environment is really great. After living in Canada, it was very easy to adapt to their culture.

Australians actually have a better sense of humour, less self-righteous. The university has a few weirdos. But then which organisation doesn't?'

Max took a sip of his wine. He gazed into the blackness of the ocean and the sky. He savoured the sweet jazz in the background swirling around the stillness of the night. He remembered those evenings in Jeddah sitting on the landing catching the sound of the same music coming up the stairs now wrapping them.

She took a sip of her wine.

'Incidentally, I was thinking about Saudi Arabia a few days ago and I realised that given where you were living in Jeddah, with no telephone, had there been an emergency while I was in boarding school, we wouldn't have been able to reach you.'

'I hadn't thought about that. You're right. But it doesn't matter, nothing happened.'

'I know but it's a bit strange.'

'I suppose,' she said, casually brushing aside the observation, as she took another sip of her wine.

Silence.

The radio station began playing Oscar Peterson's "Night Train".

'Mum, while we're talking about the past, I've been meaning to ask you this for years but there was never the right opportunity.'

'What is it, Max?'

He could tell by the ever-so-slight shifting of her body, her reaching out for her glass of wine and the almost imperceptible change in her voice that she knew Max was going to ask her about her past, his past, the many unexplained gaps in his life. It always made her uncomfortable.

'This has been bothering me for a long time. But when I lived at Mammy's, why couldn't you have taken a normal 9 to 5 job in Brussels rather than as an airline hostess, so I could have seen you every day instead of only occasionally?'

He took a long sip of his wine. Max started to fidget with his signet ring.

Silence.

'I don't know if you know how terribly sad it made me to see you leave each time. I'd cry for hours. Do you know that I still choke up today when I think about it or talk about it? And this is how deep the scar is; still today, I cannot watch the end of Mary Poppins when the children ask her whether she loved them. I have to leave the room because each time I start crying. I know it's stupid, but that's the way it is.'

Max's eyes were tearing up.

There was a long silence. Just the mellow jazz playing in the background.

'I might get us some more wine,' he said, as he got up.

She was looking away out at the blackness of the sea hoping against all hope to perhaps be able to reach out into the abyss and find an appropriate answer.

Max came back with the bottle of wine and some nuts.

'I'm very sorry Max for making you so sad, I really am,' she said, as she put her hand on his forearm and squeezed. 'And I know there is nothing I will say now that will fix that pain. I suppose I could have got a job in Brussels, but I wasn't ready to be a mum at home. I was still so young in my mid-twenties. I had got married too young, at nineteen. That's crazy.'

'But why did you marry at nineteen then? No one forced you to get married so young. If I remember correctly, you told me your father was totally opposed to that marriage for that very reason.'

'I wanted freedom to do what I wanted. I wanted freedom from my father. So, I thought that marriage was the key to that freedom, but instead, I traded one male master for another.'

Silence.

She took a sip of her wine.

'But I was so lucky that I had Mammy to look after you properly even though she certainly was not happy with the situation. Don't forget, Bonpa had only recently died. I suspect that had he still been alive I wouldn't have had that option of having Mammy look after you.'

Silence.

'Most probably not. Actually, I suspect Bonpa would have most certainly told you to take care of your own child, especially given the unusual circumstances, to put it mildly. Still, I was indeed lucky to have Mammy.'

Silence.

'The basic fact is you outsourced your responsibility to raise me to your mother.'

Silence.

'Don't you think I'm fully aware of that? I can only hope one day you will forgive me for doing this to you.'

'I hear what you are saying. But wasn't it already bad enough that you could only see Claudia on rare occasions, but you still decided willingly not to see me more often?' His voice was quivering, playing with his ring.

The Green Elevator Cage

'There's not much more I can add, Max. As I said so many times before, I needed to live a bit more before settling down to domestic life. And being an airline stewardess was exactly what I needed.'

'I see. And while we're on this difficult subject, why is it again that it took you so long, seventeen years to be exact, to tell me the truth about Claudia and her father?'

'Either there never was the right moment, or I felt that it would stir up things unnecessarily. So, I thought I might as well leave things as they were.'

'But that meant that Claudia and I were living a lie. Was it right for you to decide this?'

'I wasn't the only one. Hans also decided to keep this a secret.'

'So that made it all right, then?'

Silence. Long silence.

She took two sips of her wine.

The radio happened to be playing "Every Time You Say Goodbye," sung by Louis Armstrong. They listened to the whole song in silence.

'One last question, Mum, because I know you don't like my asking all these difficult questions but it's after all my life.'

'Sure, Max,' with the slightest hint of irritation in her voice.

Max took a sip of his wine. 'You're absolutely sure Hans isn't my father?'

'Completely certain. As certain as the sun will rise tomorrow morning!'

'Thank you, Mum. I just wanted to take this rare opportunity now that we're alone to ask you those things that have been bothering me for a long time.'

'That's absolutely fine, darling,' she said, relieved that the interrogation had finally ended.

He got up, put his hand on her shoulder and slightly squeezed it. 'What do you say, we order a pizza and watch garbage on television?'

'Great idea, Max!'

****

Canberra, 5 July 2010

Dear Claudia,

It's been so long since I last wrote you a letter. I'm very sorry about that. I hope all is fine with you. I also hope your painting is going well and that you have managed to sell a few more of your paintings. I really like them a lot!

I had to go to an academic conference in Washington ten days ago, so I decided to make a short visit to Florida to visit Mum.

It was great to see her again. I wish you had been there as well. John was not there, as he was in California visiting one of his many brothers for a week or so. Mum looked very good and in an optimistic mood as always.

As we were alone, I wanted to take the opportunity to ask her questions which had been bothering me (and probably you too!) about our/her past. Of course, it wasn't easy to do so because she hates us asking her all these 'difficult' questions. And because of that it was stressful to even ask the questions! Anyway, when I did ask her why she hadn't got a nine-to-five job in Brussels, which would have made it possible for her to see me every day when I was living with Mammy, she just said that she was too young to settle down and effectively said she still needed to have fun. And this is on top of the fact that she already had little opportunity to see you! I told her how so very sad I was each time she left me with Mammy, how my heart was shattered in so many little bits. And while she was sorry she had made me so sad, I really felt that there was very little remorse. I suppose I should just put this behind me, it's just that I'm still very sad (actually I cry) when I think of the times she would take that green elevator cage and then once again vanish.

I asked her whether she was absolutely sure that Hans wasn't my father. And she insisted that Michel was definitely my father. So, I suppose that settles that issue!

I wish you had been there to help me ask the questions. It would have been more difficult for her to avoid answering them! Anyway, I think that was the best I could hope for. I'd love to hear what you think of all that.

Here all is fine. Jane's work is going well, and Genevieve is already eleven years old. My research on Pakistan and my teaching are all going well. I'm hoping for a promotion soon.

Well, Claudia, I'd better let you go. I'd love to hear what you think of all those issues I raised with Mum.

Gros bisous,

Ton frère Max.

14

Canberra – Reunion (2015)

Max ran his eyes down the list of conference participants. They were mostly the usual suspects, people he generally didn't have much time for. He was sitting towards the back of the lecture hall on an uncomfortable chair. And then he saw her name. April Watts. He couldn't believe it. That wasn't a blast from the past, that was a thunderbolt from nowhere. The organisers had given the email details next to each participant's name. He took out his iPhone. He sent her a brief message, 'Is this the same April from Royalty Gardens? Max.' The reply was almost instant, 'Yes. But who's Max?' Max responded just as promptly, 'Max is Michel V. Meet me at the bar after conference dinner?' 'Okay!' came bursting back almost immediately.

Max looked up to try to find April. But he could only see the backs of people's heads. He typed another message, 'I'm sitting in the back, to the left. Please turn around so I know what you look like!'

A woman's head turned around about 10 rows down on the right on the other side of the aisle. She looked around briefly and their eyes locked. He waved discreetly at her. She waved back and smiled. A forty-five-year gap had just been bridged with one glance.

Max was sitting on a wooden stool at the hotel bar where the conference was being held. It was a very long, well-polished wooden bar with a gold railing in front of it.

The Green Elevator Cage

He was sipping a G&T. And then he saw April. She still had the cutest chin dimple, although it seemed a bit less pronounced than before. She was wearing a dark green, A-line skirt with a low-cut white satin top and classy high-heel white shoes. She was attractive and elegant and clearly went to the gym regularly, he thought. He couldn't believe she too would be about his age, fifty-nine.

'Well, hello Michel or is it Max?'

'Both are correct. But I'll explain later.'

They hugged each other very warmly in an attempt to recapture those lost moments of so long ago.

'I can't believe that I'm seeing you here after all those years,' Max said. 'And in Sydney of all places.'

'Neither can I. I really can't. I never thought I'd see you again. What a treat!'

They sat at the bar. They looked at each other. They smiled in disbelief, not believing what they were seeing. He could still see her on The Wall, across from him defending him against her vile brother, Sam.

'Well, where do we start? We only have forty-five years to catch up on,' she said, opening her arms in a gesture of defeat.

'I'd say, let's start by getting you a drink. What are you having?'

'I'll have a dry martini.'

'Okay, now that we each have our drinks, we can properly toast to this impromptu reunion of the former tenants of the Royalty Gardens!' Max said, with a big smile.

'Yes, to the Royalty Gardens days and to us,' April said, as they clinked their glasses.

'I suggest we each briefly summarise our past forty-five years so that we're each up to date,' Max said.

'Sounds like a good plan. You start.'

For the next ten minutes or so, Max told April about his boarding school days, his summer holidays in Mwadui, skipping Françoise, the revelation about who was his father, why he changed his name, his six years in Canada and the end of his relationship with Sophie, his university days in Brisbane, his six-month field trip to Pakistan, his failed relationship with Anne, his wife and their sixteen-year-old daughter living in Canberra.

'Wow, that's fascinating. That's quite a story and it sounds like you're happy.'

'I am. My girls are great. I'm very lucky.'

They each took a sip of their drink.

'You know, coming to Australia was probably the best thing I ever did in my life. I made mistakes in the past, but this was certainly not one of them.'

'It sounds like it.'

'As a matter of fact, I liked Australia so much from the beginning that I decided to relinquish my Green Card in 1988.'

'Wow, that's a big thing to do.'

'I know, but I felt that as I was living here and had made a life here, there was no point in keeping it. I also had to come back to the US every two years to renew it and fill income tax returns. It all became too complicated.'

'Still, as you know people pay big bucks to get their hands on one of those, legally or illegally!'

'It's funny you say that because when I went to the American Embassy to give it up, the immigration officer thought I was mad. And when I told her that I thought it was unethical to keep it, given that I was now an Australian citizen and no longer lived in the US, she said to me that she'd never heard the word ethical and green card in the same sentence! I swear to God she said that.'

'What a story!'

'I see we need another round. Do you want the same again?' Max asked.

'Sounds like a good idea.'

'Now it's your turn to tell me your life story.'

'It's not as exciting as yours.'

'I'll decide that.'

The bartender brought their drinks.

'Well, let me start with the end first. I've been working in the State Department since I left college, so almost thirty years, of working mainly in the Middle East. My last posting was in Damascus.'

Max was playing with his hotel room key. Room 827, just like the year and month he arrived in Australia, he thought.

'I understand that's a fascinating city, with so much history and beautiful art.'

'It's an incredible city,' taking a sip of her dry martini.

'You don't seem convinced when you say that.'

'I wasn't going to talk about it tonight, but now that you ask, my husband, who was also posted there with another federal agency, was shot dead there almost five years ago.'

'That's horrible! What happened?'

'Two guys on a motorcycle came close to him and shot him at close range in the head in the middle of the city. He was dead before he hit the ground.'

'I'm so sorry April!'

'It was a professional hit. And the authorities, who were probably involved in it, never found the suspects.'

'How long had you guys been married?'

'Twenty-five years, right out of college.'

'Any kids?'

'Yes, two boys, twenty-five and twenty-seven, took it pretty hard.'

'What do they do?'

'The oldest is a mechanical engineer for a big firm in South America, and the younger one is doing a PhD on Saudi Arabia. I obviously passed on my Middle East interests to him.'

'Clearly.'

'State thought it would be a good idea for me to get out of the Middle East business for a while, so I'll probably have a posting in Kuala Lumpur soon. That's why I'm here at this conference to meet some of the Australian academics working on Malaysia and the region.

'Well, at least the good thing is that we got to meet again.'

'That's true. As they say, there's a reason for everything.'

'What about the rest of your family? How are they going?'

'Well, that's a saga in its own right.'

She took a sip of her drink as if to get a boost before embarking on her story.

'To start with, my brother Sam went bad, real bad quickly, soon after we got back to the States.'

'Really?'

'You know, I still wonder how the Saudi authorities knew Sam was smoking pot.'

'I don't know. But he certainly didn't hide it, did he?' Max said, taking a sip of his G&T.'

'That's true. Still, someone must have dubbed him in.'

Silence.

They both sipped their drinks. A piano man was playing Sinatra's "Fly Me to the Moon" in the lounge area, not very far from where they were sitting.

'Do you remember this tune? Our parents used to play it at their crazy parties,' Max said, pointing his finger in the air.

'Yes, I remember. Each time I hear these songs, I think of those evenings when we would then take the opportunity to sneak out of the house,' she said.

'Yeah, and we'd meet at The Wall.'

'Anyway, back to my brother. He got mixed up with a bad crowd and got into drugs. Held up a drug store to get money to buy more drugs. He killed a cop in the process. He got thirty years in jail.'

'Wow.'

April grabbed a couple of nuts from the bowl on the bar.

'He always was a nasty piece of work. So, I'm not completely surprised he's now in jail,' Max said.

'What do you mean?'

'I don't know if you remember the Pakistani family that lived in a cardboard shack in a vacant lot next to our house.'

'Vaguely. Why?'

'Well, one day, a group of us boys were hanging around there and Sam suggested we check out the shack. So, we did. We went inside the poor people's shack and went through their very limited stuff. It was awful. All their earthly belongings were there, and we were going through them with impunity. I kept saying that this wasn't right and that we should leave. Then Sam suggested we burn the place down. We all told him that he was crazy. But he insisted and we couldn't stop him. So, with his lighter, he lit different items he found strewn around. You know, clothes that sort of stuff. The fire spread quickly and before we knew it the whole place was alight. We ran away and split up. From my house I could see into the empty lot and the shack was now really burning furiously. It took the fire engine twenty minutes to arrive. They were in no rush, as far as they were concerned, they were only Pakistanis. By the time they arrived, it was too late. The Pakistanis eventually came back to a heap of ashes. I watched the whole scene from my bedroom. It was awful, really awful. They cried; the mother could hardly hold her baby she was so distressed. Eventually, they simply walked away with what they had on their backs. Nothing else. I never saw them again.'

'That's so sad.'

'I know, and I felt so guilty, having been part of the whole thing.'

'I can imagine.'

'When I spoke to Sam about it the next day, he threatened me that if anyone found out he would kill me. And the way he said it to me, with that crazy look in his eyes, I believed him.'

'You were probably right to believe him.'

The piano man was playing "Strangers in the Night".

'Listen,' Max said, pointing to the piano man, 'another one our parents used to play.'

'I know. How crazy to think that's forty-five years ago. Where have those years gone?'

'Into thin air,' Max said, as he snapped his fingers into the air.

'Anyway, the saga gets worse. My parents divorced after returning to Chicago. My mother was tired of his philandering.'

'I'm not surprised.'

'She took my father to the cleaners. He lost pretty much everything in the divorce settlement. He started drinking, got fat, lost his job, he now lives alone in a caravan park watching porn. No woman wants to touch him.'

'Wow. And to think that he was such a suave, good-looking guy back in the nineteen-sixties.'

'Yah, a pretty big fall.'

She took a sip of her drink.

'Do you know whatever happened to the Sawyers?' Max asked.

'I heard on the grapevine that they too divorced.'

'Quelle surprise!'

'What about Jill?'

'I don't know. You know I never told you, but I was so jealous of you and Jill. I so much wanted to be the one closest to you, rather than her,' touching his forearm ever so lightly.

'But we were close. We studied a lot together and you really helped me a lot,' Max said. 'But you know having Sam as your brother would have made it very difficult to be closer.'

'I suppose you're right.'

'I can still remember all the times you told Sam to stop picking on me. I really appreciated that.'

'He was a total dickhead. And as we found out, always has been. It's in his DNA.'

'Would you like another drink?' April asked.

'Sure, why not. Lots to talk about. It's not every day you bump into an old friend.'

'That's for sure.'

'I just thought about it. Aside from my extended family, you're the person I've known the longest on this planet. I don't know what's happened to the people before Jeddah,' Max said.

'Let's toast to that milestone.'

They clinked their glasses and smiled broadly. He winked at her.

'Do you know whatever happened to Paul Johnson?'

'Yes, actually. But it's really tragic. He joined the Marines.'

'I remember that's what he wanted to do.'

'In any case, he apparently loved the travel that went with it. But sadly, he got killed in that massive terrorist bomb attack at the Marines' barracks in Beirut in 1982.'

'How do you know?'

'Working in the Middle East, I was interested in knowing who had been killed among our people. And that's when I saw his name.'

'Oh, that's so horrible,' Max said, looking away towards the piano man.

'I know, especially after what had happened to him in Jeddah.'

'Yeah, talking about getting fucked over by the Arabs twice. You know April, I can still see his bloodied, half-naked body lying there in the dirt after he had been savagely attacked in Jeddah. It was so, so horrible. And your brother making fun of it afterwards.'

'I'm so sorry, Max. It would have been so traumatic for you to see that happen to your closest friend and at such a young age.' She put her hand on his hand resting on the bar.

'...Thank you, April.'

He took a sip of his drink.

'What a schizophrenic life we lived in Jeddah! One minute we were in the middle of fucked-up Saudi society and the next we were in little America... No wonder people acted strange!'

'Yeah, no wonder.'

They spoke and laughed for another twenty minutes or so about life at the Royalty Gardens, the good, the bad and the awful.

Lightly touching Max's right forearm, she said, 'It's been so great to see you again, Max.'

'It was indeed. A real out-of-the-blue great surprise. Unless people lived in a place like Jeddah, they couldn't understand how weird it was. And to be able to share that with you was cathartic.'

'For me too. But I've got to go to bed now. The jet lag has caught up with me.'

They got up and gave each other a big, long hug.

'Are you staying at this hotel?' he asked.

'Yeah. Room 402. I thought it would be easier that way.'

'Well, I might see you at breakfast then.'

'That would be nice.'

She walked away and blew him a kiss. He waved back.

His iPhone rang. It was Jane.

'Hi, darling.'

'…Yes, the conference is pretty good, as far as they go. But you won't believe who I ran into. An old friend from Jeddah who used to live in the same compound as we did. Quite incredible. Forty-five years later. I'll have to tell you all about it when I get home tomorrow.'

'I know. It's a very small world.'

'How are things at home?'

After the phone call, Max ordered himself a cognac. He sipped it, and listening to the piano man's classic mellow music, he thought about the couple of hours he had spent with April. What a small world it is, indeed.

He finished his cognac and went to the bank of lifts.

He didn't have to wait long. Inside the lift, his hand hesitated briefly over the elevator buttons. He pressed four. The doors closed and soon reopened at level four. He stood there without moving, his heart racing. The doors closed. He stood in silence for what felt like an eternity. He pressed button eight.

15

Florida – Farewells (2015-2018)

They were all sitting around in colourful deck chairs in a rough circle by the swimming pool. Many of the 'non-skeds' had come for John's funeral and the wake at Juliette's home in Boca Raton. These were old friends of forty, or fifty years from the days of the Congo, Brussels, Beirut and various other exotic places where they had been together in good times and bad times. Many had retired in Florida, close to where Juliette and John lived. Oddly, it turned into a happy occasion for everyone to get together and reminisce about old times and wish John a happy farewell. Max had known them for most of his life. They were true friends who had stuck around and helped John and Juliette in difficult times, and there had been a few of those over the years. Max would never forget their generosity.

'So, how have you been Sam?' Max asked Sam Swabsky, a man he always associated with Beirut.

'Not too bad, all things considered.'

'That's good to hear.'

'I can't believe John has passed. It was so sudden. He always looked so fit,' Sam said.

'He was, but heart attacks can hit anyone, for no reason.'

'I know. I suppose at seventy-eight you're in the zone.'

Silence.

'He had a good and exciting life, had great friends like you and was happily married for over forty years to my mother.'

Silence.

'Yeah, you're right.'

Silence.

'Do you know I'm going to turn eighty next month?'

'Wow! Well, you sure look good for your age.'

'Thanks, Max,' taking a gulp of his scotch on the rocks.

'My great sadness is that my older brother David won't be here to celebrate my birthday.'

'Why is that?'

'He was killed on 9/11. He was in the first Twin Tower that the Arab terrorists slammed into.'

'I'm so, so sorry to hear this Sam. I didn't know.'

'What's really sad is that like me he'd survived the hell of Auschwitz but then he gets killed by Arabs in the country that gave us our freedom.'

'That's so sad Sam.'

'You know he was visiting his son Joe, my nephew, who'd just landed this job as head chef of a fancy restaurant at the very top. He was so proud of him.'

Max put his hand on Sam's forearm and gave it a bit of a squeeze. 'I'm so sorry Sam. I don't know what to say.'

'Thank you, son.'

'You know I never forgot what you told me all those years ago in Beirut about Saudi Arabia?'

'What was that again? It was so long ago.'

'Never to trust the Arabs.'

Silence.

'Yes, I remember now. You were about to leave for Saudi Arabia. We were at the airport. I was buying John's car. Cash.'

'That's right. It was at the airport.'

'Well, I guess I was right never to trust those bastards.'

The get-together had been going on for a couple of hours when Bill Bowers rose. Max remembered him well. He used to make him gin and tonics back in the Congo. Many of them. Max was only 15 but he quickly learned his trade and became the unofficial bartender whenever the pilots came around, which was often. All the guys appreciated how liberal Max was with the alcohol. Bill was originally from Texas. He had a Texan drawl and a great sense of humour. He and John had first met in Katanga in 1961 flying for the secessionist government. Later they had flown together for a dodgy outfit in Cambodia in the dying months of the Lon Nol regime. Their Convair was shot down by the Khmer Rouge but luckily, they survived that ordeal. They had gone through a lot together. A lot.

'Hey everyone. A couple of us here thought it might be nice to share some of our thoughts, stories, memories, whatever they are of John with everyone here before we all get plastered. No obligation to do so.'

For the next hour or so every pilot and navigator and each of their wives or partners shared stories of some of the flying and other adventures they had gone through with John over the last forty-plus years. Each one was funnier than the next one. Max had heard most of these stories before, as had most other people as well, he suspected. But he thought it was a great send-off for John.

Juliette became increasingly teary as more of the stories came pouring out. Max sat next to her and hugged her.

'I'm going to start crying now,' she said, as she dabbed her eyes with a tissue. 'And my mascara is going to run.'

'It's alright, Mum. You can let go. You are among friends.'

'Thank you, Max.'

After everyone had had an opportunity to say a few words, Bill rose again and offered a toast. 'To our dear friend John. You were one of the best pilots I've ever met. It was an honour, a pleasure and lots of fun to work with you over the many years in some of God's forsaken countries. May you rest in peace. Enjoy it while you can because some of us will probably join you soon.'

Everyone laughed at Bill's ability to lighten an otherwise very sad occasion. Everyone raised their glasses and joined Bill's toast.

'And if I may, Juliette dear, I'd also like to take this opportunity to remember other friends who have already left us and gone to the other side of the great divide.'

'To old friends,' they all toasted together as they raised their glasses. There wasn't a dry eye around.

****

'That was a really, great get-together yesterday, Mum. The sort of send-off John would have enjoyed.'

'You're right. And I'm sure he did wherever he's now.'

'I'm sure he did, Mum,' he said, reaching over the table to squeeze her hand.

They were at a small Italian restaurant close to where Juliette lived. It was cosy and inexpensive, and the food was good. There were many black-and-white photographs of Rome in the 1950s when women and men dressed with style and flair. They had decided to have dinner there rather than having to cook. They ordered their drinks and food. Pavarotti was singing in the background an aria from Turandot. Max was always in total bliss when listening to him.

Max was fidgeting with his signet ring.

Looking at him playing with his ring, Juliette said, 'It looks really good on you, Mammy's ring.'

'I love it. It means so much to me. It links me to Mammy and the Congo. Speaking of things from Mammy, I'm happy that Uncle Pierre finally changed his mind about Bonpa's medals.'

'Yes, that was a great surprise to get them in the mail one day.'

'Was there a note with the medals?'

'Yes, there was one. A kind one actually. He said that the more he thought about it, the more he realised that, as the oldest surviving child, I should have them so I could pass them on to you whenever I wanted to.'

'Wow, that's a big change from the wake.'

'I know. And to think that we could have avoided all that negativity had he been more reasonable on the day.'

'I suspect he wasn't himself and upset about Mammy passing away.'

'Yes, you're probably right. Still, he said things that were deeply hurtful.'

'I know but let's just forget it and move on,' Max said, reaching out to lightly squeeze her hand.

'Thank you, Max,' as she squeezed his hand in return.

They brought over their drinks. The usual dry martini for Juliette and a gin and tonic for Max. They each took sips from their drinks.

'Max, yours are so much better than this,' Juliette said, looking at her drink and putting down her glass.

'Thank you. This G&T is nothing to write home about either. Did you know people come from far and wide just for my G&Ts, and sometimes even for my company?' Max said with the usual smile appearing at the corners of his lips.

'I'm sure they do,' she said, smiling back at him and playing along with his witty remark.

Silence.

For a seventy-one-year-old, with her hair done up in a chignon, as always, she was still an attractive woman, Max thought, as he took a sip of his G&T.

'You know Pierre only wrote a very short note, wishing me well now that John was gone. I don't know why he even bothered. There was no warmth in it.'

'Look Mum, we know he never particularly liked him.'

'I know, but he could have tried just for once to be kinder about John.'

The food arrived. They ate mostly in silence, commenting once in a while on the choice of music. They ordered a second glass of red wine after the main course.

'Well, now that I have the medals, I really want you to have them.'

'That's so kind. It would mean so much to me. But are you sure you don't want to keep them, at least for a while?'

'Yes, absolutely.'

'Thank you, Mum. Thank you.'

Max reached out across the table to touch his Mum's hand. 'I love you, Mum.'

She looked up, smiling sadly, 'I love you too, so much.'

Still holding her hand, Max asked, 'With all the organising of the wake and the get-together, I haven't had a chance to properly ask you how you're going.'

'I'm fine, Max. I'm fine.'

'Mum, I know you well enough to know that you're not fine.'

Silence.

She looked sideways, away from him, her eyes tearing up.

'Mum, it wouldn't be normal if you weren't upset.'

'Forty-two years we were married. That's a lot.'

'It is.'

'And then all of sudden, poof, gone,' she said, with a click of her fingers. 'That's hard. It's so lonely in bed now, so lonely.'

Silence.

'You know I still reach out in the night to touch him but there's no one there. Just emptiness. Coldness. Nothing.'

Max squeezed her hand.

'It's so, so sad, Max.' She was now sobbing. He'd given her a tissue from his pocket.

Max looked out of the window, into the darkness. He remembered hearing sounds coming from Mum and John's bedroom one night in Jeddah. He would have been ten. It sounded like Mum was in pain, suffering. He got up. He went to their bedroom. The door was open. He stood by the door looking in. He could see silhouettes, but it wasn't clear who was whom. It was very dark. One was sitting up. He could tell that they were looking at him. Not a word was said. He didn't call out and they didn't say a word. The world froze for a long time. He didn't move. He was frozen. Eventually, he left and went back to his bedroom. They never spoke about that night's episode. But their bedroom door was shut from then on. For years he worried that John was doing bad things to his mother.

Composing herself, Juliette asked Max, 'John was good to you, wasn't he?'

'Yes, he was. But he was a bit odd and could have his difficult moments.'

'I know.'

'Like telling me when I was eight that Santa had committed suicide was a bit off.'

'Yes, that was a bit much.'

Max held his mother's aged hand. Softly caressing it with his thumb reminded him of her soft, delicate hand which would caress his teary cheeks before leaving him once again for faraway lands so long ago. The little green elevator cage was waiting. She had to go. I love you so much. Be a big boy. And she was gone. Poof. Just like that. One day she brought back a bottle of clear liqueur of some sort with a plastic ballerina inside the bottle in a glass bubble. The gracious little figure would perform pirouettes when one wound up the mechanism underneath. She would dance until the music stopped. She was a beautiful figurine, but no matter how perfectly and how long she danced she was forever imprisoned in the bottle; like Sisyphus pushing the rock up the mountain, she would be forever doomed to dance for others' enjoyment. Max wondered what had happened to that bottle.

'Mum, have you thought what you're going to do with the house?'

'I have. I've decided to sell it and move into an adult community, the same one Sam lives in. It's too difficult for me to take care of a big house and a pool by myself.'

'That's a very good idea. It's important you have an easy and relaxing time with all your friends here. They're like family. They are family.'

'Absolutely, Max. I don't know what I would do without them.'

'Are there vacancies?'

'Yes, there are a couple. But I need to move on this quickly.'

'Excellent. It would make me feel good to know that you're close to friends if you got one of these units.'

'Yes. And they're very nicely put together, and as you get older you can get extra help if you need it.'

'That's a great set-up.'

'Mum, while we're on the subject of getting all your affairs in order, you need to make sure you have an up-to-date will and a power of attorney in case anything happens suddenly.'

'Don't worry about that. Some of Hans's Swiss habits rubbed off on me,' she said, with a big grin on her face. 'That's all under control. Nothing to worry about.'

'So, your Swiss experience did bring some benefits,' Max said, with a smile on his face.

'Yes, it looks like it did indeed.'

'Shall we go? I have an early start tomorrow.'

'Good idea.' Holding back his arm, Juliette said, 'I'm so happy you could make it to John's funeral. I couldn't have done it without you. I mean it.'

'I wouldn't have missed it for anything. I wanted to be here for you.'

'I know, and I really appreciate it.'

Max thought of the lonely nights that were waiting for her.

****

There was a knock at the door of his university office. Max, who was sitting at his desk facing the gardens, turned his head around. A young woman in her early thirties, smartly dressed, wearing a blue skirt and a white linen top, was standing at the door.

'Dr Van Den Berghe?' she asked, with a charming French accent.

'Yes. What can I do for you?'

'I'm Isabelle Duval. My mother was Françoise Duval from Mwadui.'

Silence.

Rising to his feet, completely stunned, '…Please come in, please do sit down,' he said hesitantly, pointing to the empty chair by his desk.

She sat down. She was wearing white high-heeled shoes.

He immediately saw that she had the same green eyes as her mother, as well as the same warm smile.

'Well, well, I really don't know what to say. Isabelle, that's your name, right?'

'Yes, it is.'

'It's incredible to see you here in Australia. The last time I saw you, it was in Africa, and you were only four!'

'I did think you'd be surprised,' she said, with a smile, revealing a dimple in her left cheek, just like her mother.

'Where do we start? How did you find me? Are you visiting Australia? How's your mother?'

Silence.

'I'm sorry to have to break this on you after not seeing you for thirty years, but sadly my mother died recently from breast cancer. She was only sixty-two.'

'Oh… I'm so very sorry to hear this. That's really very sad.' Memories of the lush gardens at the Norfolk Hotel in Nairobi came streaming in.

Silence.

Max looked out of the window as if trying to reach out over the horizon back thirty years across time and space. He was holding back tears. He could still taste her salty tears on his lips.

'Are you alright?'

'Yes, thank you. It's just that there's so much to take in. First, the good news, seeing you, Françoise's daughter, totally unexpectedly, and then the shocking news, about your mother.' Her luscious body revealing itself slowly with every button he undid.

'I know. I'm sorry for upsetting you.'

'It's quite alright. There's never an easy way to break bad news.'

'Hopefully, this will cheer you up. I brought a picture of you and my mother.' She reached into her small, classy white purse and pulled out an envelope. She opened the flap of the envelope and pulled out a colour photograph. Françoise and he are both standing close together by a swimming pool, smiling, with a little girl in front of them. Françoise is wearing a light-yellow cotton dress and he's in shorts, bare-chested. 'In case you don't recognise me, the little girl is me. The picture isn't great. It was taken by my older brother, Didier. I was four then and he was six.'

With that thirty-year-old picture staring back at him, a jumble of memories came flooding back. 'I remember when and where that picture was taken. It was a few days before we were all going to leave Mwadui. Even though we were smiling, we were actually very sad.' The sheer bedroom curtains were undulating with the summer breeze.

Again, a long silence, as Max looked at the picture.
'You can keep the picture. I thought you'd like it.'
'Are you sure?'
'Yes, absolutely. My mother wanted you to have it.'
'Thank you so much. This means a lot to me,' as he caressed the picture hoping to bring the past back to life, like a jinni in a bottle. The noon escapades in the African bush reappeared softly.

Isabelle then reached into the envelope and pulled out a folded piece of paper.

'My mother also wanted you to have this. She said it was a poem you had written for her and given to her on the day of our departure from Mwadui.'

She handed the piece of paper to Max.

He took it and unfolded it. On the top right-hand corner, there was an imprint of red lips.

'My mother kept this poem and the picture in her wallet ever since I can remember. She kissed the poem a few days before she passed away,' Isabelle said, tears welling her eyes.

The paper had yellowed slightly, and the cursive written words had faded over the years.

'You mind if I read the poem quickly?'

'Not at all. I would be surprised if you didn't.'
He read the poem to himself.

18 August 1973

Tes yeux verts

Aujourd'hui un amour interdit,
Un amour sans espoir,
Pour toujours s'est envolé.

Tes yeux verts m'avaient enveloppé
Dans un rêve infini,
Dans un univers sans limite.

Nous avions volé des moments doux,
Des heures de tendresse
Dans la savane africaine.

Tes yeux verts m'avaient embrassé
Avec des lèvres rouges,
Des caresses d'amants intimes.

Mais toujours nous s'avions
Que le jour viendrait
Où nous devrions se dire adieu.

Tes yeux verts me quittèrent
Avec des larmes de perles,
Des larmes de tristesse.

Jamais je n'oublierai cet amour
Dans un pays lointain
Où le présent s'est arrêté pour un éternel moment.

Tes yeux verts
Seront à jamais dans mon cœur,
Toujours tes yeux verts m'accompagneront jusqu'à l'infini.

Translation from the French:

Your Green Eyes

Today, a forbidden love
A love without hope
Flew away forever.

Your green eyes had embraced me
In an infinite dream
In a limitless universe.

We had stolen sweet moments
Delicate hours
In the African savanna.

Your green eyes had kissed me
With red lips
Caresses of intimate lovers.

But always we knew
The day would come
When we'd have to bid farewell.

Your green eyes left me
with tears of pearls
Tears of sadness.

Never will I forget this love
In a faraway land
Where the present stopped for an
eternal moment.

Your green eyes
Will always be in my heart
Always your green eyes will caress me to eternity.

After reading the poem, Max folded the piece of paper. Her green eyes smiled at him warmly.

'Here, you can have the envelope and keep the photograph and the poem together as my mother had.'

'Thank you.' He could hardly look at her.

'I took the liberty of reading the poem. It's so beautiful. So tender. My mother valued it with her life.'

'Thank you for those kind words,' Max's voice breaking slightly. 'I used to write lots of poems in those days. It came so easily, almost automatic. That's all gone now.'

Silence.

'The other reason I came to see you was to pass on a message from my mother.'

'Really?'

'Yes. When she knew my husband and I were being posted to the French Consulate in Sydney, she asked me to meet with you.'

'How did she know I was in Australia?'

'She'd kept in touch with the various Mwadui friends over the years and heard on the grapevine that you had moved to Australia some time back and had become an academic.'

'Of course, the Mwadui friends.'

'So, I made a few phone calls, and it wasn't that difficult to find you.'

'Good detective work.'

'Thank you.'

'So, what was it that Françoise wanted you to tell me?'

Silence.

Isabelle took a deep breath. 'As she lay there in bed, really quite weak from her condition and all the treatments they were putting her through,' Isabelle's voice quivering ever so faintly, 'she said to tell you that even though you had gone silent on her once you had left Mwadui in 1973, she never held it against you. She understood why. She also said to tell you that those summer months were the happiest days of her life which she would always treasure to her dying days.'

Long silence.

She looked away at the bookshelves to her left and Max looked down at her white shoes. He caressed his signet ring.

Hearing those words from Isabelle, almost directly from Françoise herself, was too much for Max. This time he couldn't hold back the tears. He turned away. His eyes filled with tears and now they silently rolled down his cheeks. He took a tissue from the Kleenex box on his desk and discreetly dried his cheeks. The DC-3 was fast-losing height, the end was near.

Without turning back to Isabelle, he mumbled, 'I'm sorry. I'm really sorry about this.'

'Please, don't be. I'm not surprised by your reaction. I know that you were very close for those few months back in Mwadui.'

'We were indeed,' Max muttered, still looking away, facing the garden. Their wet bodies enlaced in the heat.

'I really believe that now that I've passed on her message, she can rest in peace. It was something she really wanted me to do because it meant so much to her.'

'You're probably right,' as he turned back to face her.

'I'm going to have to go now because I've got to catch a flight back to Sydney.'

The Green Elevator Cage

'Of course, I understand. Now that I know you live in Sydney, next time you come to Canberra we must have lunch. Promise?'

'That's a great idea. You can then tell me all about Mwadui. I've only heard Mum's version; I'd love to hear yours.'

'Okay, that's a deal.'

They both got up.

'I know it's assuming a lot, but would you terribly mind if I gave you a hug?' Max asked.

'Of course not. I was hoping you would ask. We do go back thirty years after all,' she said, with the sweetest smile on her face.

They hugged warmly.

'Thank you so much for making the effort to come and see me. This has meant a lot to me. A lot.'

'For me too. And for Françoise, of course.'

'Of course.'

He heard Isabelle's footsteps going down the corridor. They echoed down the hallway like memories drilling deep into his heart. He shut the door to his office and sat down at his desk. He took out his wallet from his back pocket and tucked away in one of its small folds he took out the 1941 One French Franc Françoise had given him on the last day in Mwadui. Holding it in his hand brought back Françoise's departing words in Nairobi he would never, ever forget: 'Adieu, Michel, mon amour. Adieu'. And those words would always be accompanied by Roberta Flack's "Killing Me Softly with His Song".

He looked out of the window, saw a Crimson Rosella land on a branch just outside his window, and then he cried as he hadn't since he had ripped up Françoise's unread, unopened last letter so long ago.

****

Max received a letter from Claudia in early July 2009. They didn't write to each other that often, so when he did get a letter, other than for his birthday or Christmas, it was usually because there was something important she wanted to talk about. He would add the Swiss stamp to his collection.

Zurich, 12 July 2009

My dearest Max,

I was going to give you a call instead of writing a letter, but I thought it was probably best this way.

My father died last week. It was not totally unexpected, but it was still very sad to see him go. He was seventy-nine. That's not that old.

As you know, my father had been quite ill for a long time. His heart was poor. And he knew it that's why he had all his affairs put in order years back. I know it was a bit strange for you to have to go to the Swiss Embassy to sign those legal papers. But I'm sure you understand.

I had a complicated relationship with my father. I loved him dearly. He always loved me. I know that. But he allowed my stepmother to come in between us. She often tried to divide us, sometimes even using my half-brother and two half-sisters to help out. So, my father and I could only be close when we were alone. It was a sad situation, but I had to accept that.

The Green Elevator Cage

My stepmother had never hidden that she always thought I was a hindrance to her family life. She made that very clear from day one. She also didn't hide her preference for her children. So, as you know, as soon as I turned eighteen, I left home to live away from my stepmother. My father kindly helped me financially at the beginning. He was sad to see me go, but he understood why it was probably best for all. We would meet once a week for lunch, and those were my happiest times with my father. And we had these lunches until quite recently. I will dearly miss those special moments.

The only thing I will always regret is that he never wanted to talk to me about Mum. Never. It was as if the first marriage had never happened, that Mum had never existed, except that each time he saw me reality hit him. So, when I left the house, I suspect things got easier for him in the home.

I know my father meant nothing to you, and I understand that. Why would he? But I wanted to share a few of my thoughts about him. As you know, he wasn't a bad man. He simply never completely recovered from the shipwreck that was his first marriage.

I'm going to write to Mum now to also let her know. But I don't think she'd be very interested. Why would she be? The whole marital experience was a disaster.

I hope all is well with you. I'm sure your two 'girls' are spoiling you. I can't believe that Genevieve is already 15. How time flies!

Gros bisous de ta grande sœur. xxx

Claudia

Max read the letter a couple of times. He thought how sad she would have to be now. He remembered how horrible her stepmother had been towards her, telling her that she would never love her because she wasn't her daughter. This was straight out of a Grimm Brothers fairy tale. But the good news was that she got along with one of her half-sisters. Thank God for small mercies, he thought.

Even though the death of Hans should mean nothing to him, Max felt something, but he wasn't quite sure what. Maybe it was that home movie seeing Hans playing with him not knowing he wasn't his son but his colleague's. And to think that until the age of seventeen, he thought he was his father. What lies so many of us live.

****

One morning in late winter 2010, Max found the male resident magpie dead in his garden. He recognised it right away: it had this feather that stuck out at a strange angle. It was still warm. He could see his dead canary at the bottom of the cage, Mammy in the coffin. Stillness. Sadness. His female partner-for-life was distressed, as was their one-year-old juvenile. They were walking around, not knowing what to do but knowing what had happened. She'd have to find a new male partner fast, or she would be turfed out by marauding magpies on the lookout for new rich feeding grounds for spring. And with all the native plants, the rich soil, the bird food and the clean birdbath, this was prime real estate. They had been continuously under attack by magpies trying to muscle in. The juvenile had no chance of staying. It was brutal.

Given that magpies live up to twenty years, he would have been on the property as long as him, Max thought. He buried the magpie in his garden at the foot of the massive gum tree, where it probably was born in a nest some twenty metres above many years earlier. A new crop of magpies would soon be raised, and life would continue. Max loved them all.

16

Brussels – La Grand'Place (2018)

'Que puis-je vous offrir?' the waiter asked, as he wiped down the table. He was wearing the usual brown leather apron that all waiters wore Au Roy d'Espagne, the most popular café on Brussels's famous Grand'Place. Their uniform hadn't changed in 100 years.

'I'll have a white wine,' said Jane.

'And I'll have an apple juice,' said Genevieve.

'On aura un vin blanc, un jus de pomme et une Leffe, s'il vous plait,' said Max to the waiter.

'Pas de problème. Monsieur.'

'I can't believe we're here in Brussels. The three of us together,' Max said to Jane and Genevieve.

They were sitting on the terrace. The weather was perfect for a July afternoon. The sun was out and there was only a very slight breeze. As one would expect, the Grand'Place was seriously crowded with many tourists from all over the world. Most were taking selfies, probably the most self-absorbed activity of the twenty-first century. In my kingdom, they would be banned, and their users banished to another country, thought Max.

Max felt good. His two favourite women were here with him. He hadn't been back to Brussels for any length of time for some forty years. But now here he was with his family so many years later. They had arrived in Brussels only two days ago.

'I can't wait to show you guys around my old haunts.'

'It'll be great, Dad, to have you show all those places you've talked to us about over the years.'

'I can't even tell you how many times I've come to this café we're at now. I can still remember coming here when I was only six or seven. The stuffed horse inside was already there. And it shows too!'

'Yes, it does look old,' Genevieve said.

'People are funny. As you see, there are many other similar cafés in this square, but everyone flocks to this one even though the others serve exactly the same beer,' Max said to no one in particular.

Jane had been posted as the Australian Ambassador to Belgium, Luxembourg, NATO and the EU. This was not only a great diplomatic posting, but it was also an opportunity for Max to live in Brussels, a city which had been on and off so important to him in the first twenty years of his life.

They enjoyed their drinks, with Max pointing and commenting at various things on the square, telling them anecdotes of things that had happened to him on the square so many years ago.

'Okay guys, shall we go and have a bite to eat for lunch? There's a restaurant I'd like to bring you to which is very special to me.'

They walked the ten-minute stroll to the Rue des Bouchers where Chez Léon was located. He knew exactly how to get there even though he hadn't been there in decades. It was as if the layout of Brussels had been hardwired into Max's brain. The cobblestones were still there, as were all the chocolatiers and embroidery shops. This was after all the tourist Mecca of Brussels. The restaurant was a Brussels institution which had been there for the last eighty years, at least. Everyone knew Chez Léon.

The waiter, who wore the traditional black apron with front pockets, sat them at a table for four. All the tables had red and white chequered tablecloths.

'So, why is this restaurant so special to you, darling?' asked Jane.

'This is where my mother, Claudia and I had lunch in 1969. I was thirteen. I hadn't seen Claudia since we had been separated when I was two. I can still remember that day as if it was yesterday. We sat there,' as Max pointed to a table on the same floor.

'That's incredible, Dad. It must have been really emotional to see your sister again after all those years. For the first time, really.'

'…It was darling. It really was,' looking at the table trying to recapture that special moment. 'We couldn't stop talking about everything and nothing. We had so much to catch up on, as you can imagine. So much time lost.'

Max started to choke. He had to stop talking because he could sense that he'd start to shed tears. There were few things which made him cry in life but thinking of that long sibling separation saddened him deeply. His mother going off on her many trips and leaving him behind when he was a little boy was another deep cut. Both of these were so deeply embedded in his soul, there was nothing he could do. Just nothing. The scars had simply never completely healed, and probably never would.

'Oh, poor darling.' Jane tried to console Max. Sitting next to him, she leaned over and hugged him tightly. Genevieve leaned over and held his hand.

'I'm fine girls. I'm sorry. It's so silly after so many years but I simply cannot help it.'

'You mustn't be sorry, darling.'

'We better order guys,' he said.

The rest of the lunch went smoothly. Max told them stories of Brussels and what he had been up to as a teenager. They all had a good time, as they ate away at their moules-frites.

'I'd like to go to the coast for the day one of these days and check it out. I'd like to try to remember what it was like to go there with Mammy and Uncle Pierre during the summer holidays.'

'You should darling,' Jane said, as she pressed his hand.

'Thank you for indulging me'

'Don't be so silly.'

Max kept on eating his meal, thinking of those days so long ago when he used to play in the dunes with friends he would have made during the holidays. He wondered what had ever happened to them. Did they wonder what had happened to him?

'Are you okay, Dad?'

'Yeah, of course, I was just daydreaming darling. All good.'

17

Florida – Adieu!
(2019)

Max and Claudia were standing side by side looking down at the open coffin in front of them at the funeral parlour. Their mother had died quite suddenly from a brain tumour. She was eighty-six. Just like with Mammy, Max didn't really recognise his dead mother. He thought how strange it was that once the soul is gone, the body becomes an empty shell devoid of personality, a mere cadaver.

The sound of Albinoni's Adagio in G Minor was whiffing through the room, enveloping them softly. It was a sound he knew well, having heard it hundreds of times at boarding school at the beginning of virtually every mass. Albinoni had really cornered the market on this event. The tan-coloured walls were sparingly covered with large photographs of sunsets. Max thought that these were poorly chosen given that the sun would have already long set on anyone in a coffin. It would have been better to have abstract paintings. It was all surreal really, he thought. One day you're alive and the next day you're gone. Pouf. Gone.

According to the managers of the old age caring home, she'd been living at for the last 15 years since John had passed away, she'd been behaving quite erratically of late. About a month earlier, she'd had a bad fall going to the dining room and had banged her head quite hard. They brought her to the hospital to put her under close observation and that's when they discovered that there were three malignant tumours deeply embedded in her brain. These were inoperable. They were surprised that she could still function. However, the fall had accelerated the decline quite dramatically. So much so that within four days she was dead.

Neither Max nor Claudia was able to get to Florida before she passed away. Instead, they had to look at an empty shell, silently, deeply saddened that they had been unable to say some final words to their mother. As he looked at his mother, Max thought of the many painful departures he'd had to live through as a little boy each time she flew off to exotic lands. And now this departure was permanent. The green elevator cage would never bring her back. He had loved her so much, but she had made him so sad so many times. And what hurt him most was that she seemed to have been completely oblivious to it. She'd never really apologised or understood what painful impact all her departures had had on him then, and how, so many years later, he had still never quite got over it.

Max had silent tears running down his cheeks. He put out his right hand and Claudia took it. They held hands for a few minutes. They then hugged each other.

'I'm so sad, Claudia,' Max said softly into her ear.

'I know Max. I know,' as she patted his back.

'She's taken so many unanswered questions and secrets with her.'

'I know. And we'll never have the answers to them. We'll have to accept that,' almost whispering into Max's ear.

'You're absolutely right,' Max said, as he wiped his tears with a tissue. 'I think we should go.'

'Yes, I think so.'

****

The group of "non-skeds" had thinned out quite significantly since the last big together for John's wake. Still, there were enough of the old friends to make the wake for his Mum respectable enough, Max thought. Sadly, Sam had joined John on the other side some years back. They were all sitting in a sort of circle close to the swimming pool at Juliette's aged care home. Even though it went against house policy, management had decided to allow them all to have alcoholic beverages for this special occasion. It wasn't every day that old friends got together to say farewell to one of theirs.

Max was happy to see that Bill Bowers had been able to make it. And for someone who was ninety-one, he looked pretty good. Like Sam, Bill had always been special to Max. He would never forget how Bill had taught him how to shuffle a deck of cards like a pro at the bar of the Normandie Hotel in Beirut. He was only nine years old. This special acquired skill had impressed his friends at boarding school but not so much the priests, especially on the day he had been caught by the headmaster gambling in the school chapel. Comparing himself to Jesus booting the merchants out of the temple, the headmaster kicked Max out of the chapel. However, it was when Max asked the headmaster if he could first play his hand that he really got upset. It cost him a weekend detention. Still today, when Max thinks of God, which isn't often, he thinks of the winning hand he never got to play.

'It's so good to see you here, Bill,' Max said, putting his arm around him in a warm embrace.

'Juliette was a very special person. I wouldn't have wanted to miss this last goodbye.'

'I know. I know.'

'Quite frankly, I'm surprised she put up with so much shit from John,' Bill said.

'Yes, he could be difficult. But on the whole, he was a pretty good guy.' Max took a sip of his G&T.

'Yeah, I suppose you're right.'

Max turned to Claudia who was sitting next to him, 'How are you going there?'

'I'm fine,' she smiled.

'I know you don't know any of these people, but they are like family. I have known them ever since I was a little boy, hearing about their adventures, making them drinks, and sharing my stories. They loved Mum.'

'I can see that they mean a lot to you.'

'They do. You know there were so many more of them at one point, but many have moved on, perhaps to a better place, who knows.'

Using his cane, Bill got up, and standing unsteadily on his feet, he said, 'Okay guys, I think this is a good time to say a few words about Juliette. As we did with John, we'll go around, and if anyone has anything to say, this will be their opportunity to do so.'

Everyone said a few words, with most of them joking about her thick but charming Belgian accent. Many of them spoke of her great ability to adapt easily to all the different places they had lived. But what most impressed them was Juliette's management of John's not-always-easy personality.

It was Max's turn to say a few words. He took a couple of gulps of his drink. He looked at the swimming pool, slightly mesmerized by the blueness of the water. He remembered when he lived in Jeddah when they'd go to what they called the 'Creek', an inlet from the Red Sea. It was the expatriates' getaway by the water. It was very rudimentary with a few wooden shacks. But it was a great way to get away from the city and go into another bubble. His mother would have been in her mid-thirties and clearly very attractive. Max never forgot how each time his mother would get up to go to the water for a swim, all the men, particularly those with wives and children by their side, would unashamedly turn their heads to check her out. And it certainly wasn't her chignon which got all these men's attention.

As a little boy, he always thought his Mum was the most beautiful woman in the world. There was no competition. Later, he thought of her as a combination of the elegance of Catherine Deneuve and the beauty of Julie Christie. She was also very charming but surprisingly, often she had no clue about some things in life or was disarmingly flippant about others. But she got away with it because of her inherent charisma.

Max told them about the time a few weeks before leaving Mwadui when she'd asked him to bring their German shepherd to potential new owners so they could get to know him. Max had said that this was a very bad idea because these people had a Dachshund which would not be happy to see a big dog enter his territory. 'Oh, don't worry about it,' she said, 'it'll all be fine.' 'Well, it turned out not to be fine; actually, it turned out to be a disaster,' Max said. The German shepherd managed to get out of his leash, and it savagely destroyed the much smaller dog which was determined to defend his home turf. The last thing Max remembered was seeing the Dachshund being swung into the air, and then falling hard on its side. The poor dog, yelping, managed to crawl away and hide under the kitchen table. It eventually died a couple of days later of a punctured lung. 'Needless to say, the potential new owners decided not to take our German shepherd. Mum didn't seem to care too much really of what had happened to the Dachshund. And typical of her reaction, which was quite ruthless at times, she said, 'He was an ugly little dog anyway.' I reminded her that these people actually loved that ugly little sausage dog. 'Well, maybe but he shouldn't have tried to fight our German shepherd, that was stupid.'

Everyone thought this was a very funny story and typical of Juliette's approach to life, carefree, nonchalant, and not too worried about the consequences of her actions.

'Let's all toast to Juliette,' Bill said, as he raised his glass. 'May she continue to have a good time on the other side with John, with a ready supply of dry martinis, of course!'

Everyone agreed, raised their glasses and in unison cried out, 'To Juliette!'

****

The residential community was a sprawling single-storey structure. Its name was above the main entrance in large, golden letters: RENAISSANCE. Max always thought that whoever had come up with that name had a sick sense of humour or didn't know what the French word meant. But he was sure that all occupants knew exactly what the score was; there was no re-birth once you passed the front door, only a wait to cross the great divide into the abyss, hopefully not too painful.

The manager of the establishment was a woman in her fifties with too much make-up and teeth which were simply too white to be natural. She welcomed Claudia and Max into her office and invited them to sit down on the two chairs in front of her large wooden desk as she proceeded to sit behind it.

'I am so sorry about the passing of your mother. Please accept my deepest condolences,' she said, affecting well the appearance of genuinely caring.

'Thank you,' Max and Claudia said in unison.

'She was such a lovely and happy person, with a great sense of humour. She had so many friends. Everyone loved her. She was unique.'

'Yes, she was a very warm and unique person in so many ways,' Max said.

'Let me just say that she doesn't seem to have suffered much. It all happened very quickly.'

'That's good to hear,' said Claudia in a subdued voice.

'If it's okay with you, I'd like to briefly discuss the issue of disposing of your mother's belongings and then you can visit her living quarters at your leisure.' A white smile ran across her face.

'Of course,' Max said.

'Juliette gave us instructions that whatever you didn't want to take should either be sold or be given to charity. And, of course, we will take care of that side of things. So, you need not worry about that. It's all part of our fully integrated services that we provide to the families of our community,' she said, breaking into another artificial white smile.

'Thank you for that. That's very helpful,' said Claudia.

'You're really quite welcome. Needless to say, we will also take care of the cremation process, which should take place tomorrow, if that works for you?'

'That's fine. That too would help us a lot,' Max said.

'I believe that's all I have to say for now. Do you have any questions?'

'I don't have any,' said Max. 'Do you?' turning to Claudia.

'No,' she almost whispered, gently nodding her head.

'Let me walk you to Juliette's apartment then,' the manager said, rising from behind her desk.

They walked down the tan-carpeted hallway, with the manager slightly ahead of them. She was wearing high-heel, black lacquer shoes. Max always wondered how women managed to walk with such unnatural contraptions without twisting their ankles or simply falling over. The hallway was well-lit, with small lights over each occupant's nameplate to the left of each door. All doors were shut and there was no one to be seen in the hallway. There was a clinical smell of lavender in the air. That lifeless, pictureless corridor reminded Max of a book he had read back in the early 1980s called 'Prisoner Without a Name, Cell Without a Number' about a Jewish political prisoner in Argentina. They stopped at door number forty-two. Of all numbers did it have to be that one, Max thought.

The manager opened the door and walked in. 'Except for tidying up, we left everything as it was when she passed. I'm going to leave you now. Please take your time.

There's absolutely no rush. And, of course, if there is anything I can do please don't be afraid to ask.' Another white smile crossed her face. And then she was gone.

Max and Claudia looked at each other, not sure what to do.

'Almost twenty-five years ago, we went through the same thing with Mammy. A whole life reduced to a few faded, worn, forgotten items,' Max said, looking around.

'I know. It's so sad.'

The living room was relatively large, with a small kitchenette in the corner, partly hidden by a high white marble counter. There was a comfortable-looking couch and a large television facing it. Above the couch, two of Claudia's paintings were hanging. Next to the couch, there was a traditional reclining leather armchair. Max suspected that's where his Mum must have been whiling away her last years, watching meaningless garbage on television, neither looking nor absorbing. There was a large, free-standing, two-door, wooden wardrobe in the far corner. Max recognised it immediately; John and Mum had kept it for at least thirty years. The bedroom and on suite were to the right of the entrance. It was comfortable and appropriately set up for ease of movement.

'Let's have a look at what's in the wardrobe,' Claudia suggested.

'Good idea.'

And just as when they opened the old green metal trunk in Mammy's room some twenty-five years earlier, opening the wardrobe revealed, like Ali Baba's cave, lost treasures.

'Wow, look at all this mixed bag of stuff!' Max said, trying to make sense of what was in front of them.

'I know, there's such an eclectic collection of things. Where do we start?'

'Why don't we look at things, and anything we'd like to keep, we can agree who keeps it. If there is too much to take with us in our suitcases, we can always have management organise to have it sent to us back in Switzerland and Australia,' Max said.

'That's a very good idea.'

For the next two hours or so, they went through all the items in the wardrobe. Quite a bit was useless, junk collected from faraway lands over the years, Max thought, but some had real sentimental value.

'Look at this, Claudia.' Max was holding a bundle of letters from the Belgian Congo tied together with a wide red ribbon, all from Mum to Mammy. Some had been written from Elizabethville to Mammy in Leopoldville and some later from Leopoldville to Mammy in Brussels. 'Let's take these with us and read them at the restaurant tonight. We may learn a thing or two which she never told us.'

'Yes, I'm sure these letters will reveal things. She must have taken these with her from Mammy's treasure trove twenty-five years ago,' Claudia said.

'She must have. If you don't mind, I'll have to keep the stamps for my collection.'

'Of course, those stamps will mean that much more to you.'

They went back to their search, looking for nothing in particular, but hoping to find some more interesting paraphernalia. And then Max saw the framed photograph. It was the picture that had been taken with his Kodak 104 camera at the Brussels restaurant Chez Léon when they were all reunited for the first time fifty years ago.

'Look at us, Claudia. We all looked so happy. I'll organise to have a duplicate made of it because there is no way that Mum would still have the negative. We each have to have a copy of it.'

'That would be great if you could do that.'

They returned to their foraging.

'Oh, look, Max, a flacon of Mum's favourite perfume. I'd like to take that with me.' Opening the small bottle, she delicately brought it to her nose and smelt it. 'You know that scent is the way I always remember Mum. She was that scent. It was unique to her,' smiling at me. 'Here smell it,' holding the flacon out for Max to smell it. 'I know what you mean,' as he too smelt it. 'You know she told me that she couldn't smell it anymore.'

'I'm not surprised. If you wear the same perfume for sixty years, it becomes a part of you.'

And then Max saw Mum's famous fountain pen which she had had ever since he could remember. From that fountain pen, Max thought, Mum created all those green characters that adorned the hundreds of letters he received from her at boarding school and elsewhere.

'Would you mind if I took the fountain pen? It means a lot to me.'

'Of course not.'

They continued rummaging through the wardrobe for another hour or so. As they were getting towards the end of their exploration, they found Juliette's wallet in the very back of the wardrobe. It was black leather, worn over the many years of use. Max couldn't remember when she'd had another one.

'I know it's silly, but I feel bad opening it,' Max said.

'I know what you mean.'

He opened it, and in it were many credit cards and about a dozen membership cards to book clubs, gym clubs, wine retailers and other shopping venues all neatly placed in their individual slots. As they took them out one by one, they saw that most of the cards had expired years earlier. As he kept investigating the various other compartments of the wallet, with Claudia by his side, he felt something tucked deep inside one of the pockets.

'I can feel something else in there, sticking to the inside. It feels like a picture, but it's stuck. It must have been in there a long time.'

'Let me have a go. It might be easier with my fingernails.'

Max handed the wallet to Claudia so she could have a go at retrieving it. It didn't take long before she was pulling out an old black and white photograph. Holding it in her fingers, Claudia brought it closer to Max and they both looked at it together. They immediately knew what it was.

'My God, it's a picture of Michel!' Max said, totally shocked. Immediately, he thought of the One French Franc in his wallet Françoise had given him so long ago.

'Unbelievable!' Claudia said, almost simultaneously, turning the photograph over. On the back was written: "Juliette, je t'adore. xxx Michel."

Max and Claudia looked at each other in total disbelief. Speechless.

'Do you think she's had a picture of Michel in her wallet for well over sixty years?' Max asked, still in shock at the discovery.

'…I don't know. I really don't know. Quite possibly,' Claudia said, stuttering her words.

'Wow. He must have really meant a lot to her to keep a picture of him all these years,' Max said, looking at Michel who was sitting at a table smiling broadly at the camera. He is wearing a light-coloured linen suit. There are two martini glasses on the table. An African waiter standing in the background. The photograph must have been taken at a bar either in Leopoldville or Elizabethville, Max thought.

'He must have. And to think she kept that secret to herself the whole time. Amazing.'

'I still can't believe it. Anyway, let's wrap up things here. We can talk about this later,' Max said.

They agreed to share the photo albums, various other pictures, and the African masks. They each took a Middle Eastern rug. They agreed with management for the rest to be either sold or given to charity as requested by Juliette. The heavy items would be shipped to them in the next few weeks.

Standing outside the community below the RENAISSANCE sign, Max said, 'I think we should go for dinner and read all the letters Mum wrote to Mammy.'

'Yes, that's a great idea. You know where to go?'

'I do, indeed.'

****

That evening Claudia and Max went to the same Italian restaurant he had gone to with their mother after John's death. Not much had changed, if anything. They were still playing the same operatic arias; the black and white pictures had faded considerably, the red and white tablecloth looked tired, and the same owners had aged poorly.

'What brings you here?' asked the owner.

'Sadly, my sister and I have just been to our mother's wake. I came here with our mother when her husband died fifteen years ago. And I remember that the food was appetising.'

'I'm very sorry to hear about the passing of your mother. She used to come here regularly with some of her friends from the adult community she lived at. A lovely lady with a great accent.'

'Thank you. She never did lose that thick Belgian accent.'

'It made her very charming. So, what can I get you guys to start with?'

Turning to Claudia, Max asked, 'Shall we get a bottle of red wine, something not too heavy?'

'Sounds good.'

'Okay, we'll have a Pinot Noir or something like that, please. I'll let you choose one for us,' Max said to the owner.

'I have a Californian red that I'm sure you'll like a lot. I'll be right back.'

Silence.

Max looked around, then at Claudia.

'So here we are at our mother's funeral fifty years since we first really met in Brussels. It's difficult to believe it was so long ago,' Max said.

'I'll never, ever forget that moment on the station platform. It was so beautiful, all hugging each other,' Claudia's eyes were tearing up.

'Nor will I,' he said, taking her hand. 'I'm so happy we could both make it to Mum's funeral,' choking up.

'Me too. It's good we could both say goodbye together.'

'Listen, they're playing one of my favourite arias sung by Pavarotti, my favourite tenor,' he said, putting his index up in the air. 'La Bohème. When I hear him sing, so deeply, so powerfully from the heart, I feel like crying. Probably the best of all tenors, ever.'

Max looked away.

The waiter brought the bottle of wine and poured some into each glass.

They ordered their food but told the owner that there was no rush.

Once alone, Max and Claudia, almost simultaneously, picked up their glasses and raised them.

'To Mum,' they toasted, smiling with their eyes.

'You know, I can still remember that little tin box with all your treasures which you kept hidden behind the books in the large bookshelf in the dining room in Brussels. You brought it over to where we were sitting on the couch, delicately opened it and showed me that adorable picture of us in the Belgian Congo.'

'You know, I still have that little tin box. My most sentimental things are in it.'

Max took a sip of his wine.

'Let's read Mum's letters to Mammy,' Claudia said, in an excited voice.

'Great idea. Let's read them now while we're waiting for our food,' Max said.

Claudia took the bundle out of her bag and put them in the middle of the table. There were about twenty letters. Max took the first one on the top. He took the letter out of the envelope. It was from Elizabethville, dated April 1954. He opened it and put it in the middle so they could both read it at the same time, like children reading a kid's storybook. Surprisingly, it was written in French, not in Flemish, probably more out of habit rather than anything else, Max thought.

Elizabethville, 25 April 1954

Dear Mammy,

I hope you, Bonpa and Pierre are all well.

I wanted to write you a short note to send you a couple of pictures of Claudia.

It's quite amazing to think that Claudia is already one year old today. She's growing so quickly and becoming more beautiful by the day. She can almost walk. She furniture-walks really, moving from the chair to the table to the sofa, holding to the items before making a move on her wobbly legs to the next item. But she doesn't always make it and then falls on her behind. But with all her nappies, she doesn't feel it!

Even though I have domestic help, Claudia keeps me busy all day. Every day is a new day of discovery for her and for me!

Here all is going well. I can't believe that it has already been two years since I got married. How time flies! Hans is very good to me, but he's gone all day at the office. And I don't have that many friends, not like when I lived in Leopoldville. Sometimes he's gone for several days to follow up on projects his Swiss company is involved in. I get lonely then. But he always brings me a small present on his return. I love that.

Well, I'd better close this letter.

I love you so much and miss you even more.

xxx Juliette.

'It's fascinating to get a glimpse into Mum's life more than sixty years ago!' Max said.

'I know, especially that she never spoke about it. But you know what is great is that because I went to Lubumbashi with you and John in 1972, I can better imagine how life would have been.'

'You would.'

'Do you think we have time for another before they bring us dinner?' Max asked.

'We can always start.'

'Let's get one further down the pile. How about this one,' as Max pulled a letter out. It was postmarked Leopoldville, dated July 1955.

Leopoldville, 16 July 1955

Dear Mammy,

I hope you and Pierre are well.

I can't believe it's been four months since I was in Brussels for Bonpa's funeral. I'm still so sad that he's no longer with us. It also saddens me that when I last spoke to him in Leopoldville, we had a big fight over my marriage to Hans. That was such an awful way to say goodbye. I didn't know I'd never see him again alive. I feel so, so bad about it all.

I hope you and Pierre are adjusting okay in Brussels without Bonpa. It wouldn't be easy.

On a totally different subject, I've got big news: I'm pregnant! Claudia should have a little brother or sister in early February next year. The doctor confirmed it. This was quite unexpected. I've told Claudia but I don't think she quite understands what it all means. Claudia will be almost three when her sibling arrives. She's so beautiful and so much fun to have around.

I'm happy to be back in Leopoldville where I have many more friends and there are so many more social activities to go to, including lots of parties. Elizabethville was such a dump, with nothing to do. My only worry is that Hans wants to go back to Zurich sooner than later. He hadn't told me this before we got married. I thought he wanted to stay here in the Congo as long as possible. I hated it when we were there for our wedding. They all spoke in Swiss German, which I couldn't understand. They didn't like me, especially his mother, because I wasn't a girl from their village. It was awful. Also, I had to clean my own bathroom and make my own bed. Life is so much easier in the Congo. Hopefully, he will change his mind about that silly idea of his.

Well, I'd better close this letter so I can send it off to you. I hope all is well with you and Pierre. I do miss Bonpa so much.

Lots of love,

xxx Juliette

The food arrived. They each had pasta. They ate mainly in silence.

When the main course was finished, Max recalled how wonderful it had been to see her and their mother at his sixtieth birthday party in Brussels three years earlier. It had been quite an evening. It was black tie dress code, with a live jazz trio, and excellent food made at the Residence by the Finnish chef. Given the tension between the various members of the extended family, he had decided not to invite any of them. It was much easier that way; everyone could be equally upset. He had invited several diplomats and their spouses. He would have liked to have seen more of his personal friends from Australia, but he could hardly expect them to fly across half the world just for a birthday party.

'Yes, it was really lots of fun, Max. You know some really interesting people.'

'I never thought I'd ever be celebrating my sixtieth!'

'I know you don't like ageing but that's simply like that. Look, I'll always be older than you. That should make you feel better,' she said, with a smile on her face.

'That's true, but of small comfort,' Max said.

He took a sip of his wine.

'You know what I really liked most about my stay in Brussels was going with Mum and you to where you grew up with Mammy so long ago,' Claudia said.

'I know that was the highlight of our get-together with Mum. It meant a lot to me. It was like a pilgrimage.'

'And we were so lucky that when we got to Mammy's old place, there were these young people outside the main door. And they happened to be living in the apartment you used to live in.'

'And wasn't it nice of them to let us go up with them to have a quick look at the apartment?' Max said.

Max poured some more wine into each glass.

'You know going up in that lift, a green cage really, to the fourth floor really brought back so many sad memories. My heart was really pounding so hard. It was in my throat.'

Silence.

The Green Elevator Cage

'It made me think of all the times Mum would leave me when I was just a little boy, wanting to be with her.'

'Oh Max,' Claudia said, as she warmly patted his hand. 'I'm so sorry.'

'I should stop going on about it. I was the lucky one. You hardly got to see her as a little girl, and with a horrible stepmother to boot.'

'I know, but I had my father. And that helped a lot.'

'As you know, I've forgiven her. She was just so young. But the pain never really left me, ever. It's so deep.'

'I know Max,' Claudia patted his hand again.

'Thank you, big sister,' Max said, with a jagged smile.

Max poured the rest of the wine into each glass.

'When I finally saw the inside of the apartment, it felt so small,' Max said.

'You were a small boy after all when you left.'

'It was strange to see the room I slept in, next to Mammy. And the wall where Bonpa's medals were hanging now had a picture of a Van Gogh painting. How funny is that?'

'I remember the living room where you told me about the game of Monopoly with John and how it all went badly wrong.'

'Yes, it was really special for me. Mum didn't say very much during the visit. I suppose she was trying to take it all in.'

'It was after all a bit of an emotional rollercoaster going back. And don't forget Max, I'm sure she wouldn't have enjoyed leaving you with Mammy each time. I'm sure her heart was also crying.'

'You're absolutely right, Claudia.'

'I think we should order another drink. What would you like?' Max asked.

'I'll have a cognac.'

'That's exactly what I was thinking of getting.'

Pavarotti was singing an aria from Puccini's Turandot. Impeccable timing, Max thought.

'I adore this opera,' Claudia said, closing her eyes to better listen.

After the two cognacs arrived, Max suggested they read a couple more letters. The next one was also from Leopoldville.

Leopoldville, 15 May 1956

Dear Mammy,

I hope you and Pierre are well.

Just a quick note to send a couple of pictures of Claudia and her little brother Michel. She adores him. She thinks he's a doll for her to play with. But because he sleeps most of the time, she gets a bit upset that he doesn't want to play.

Hans keeps talking of wanting to move back to Zurich. We've had real big fights over it. I'm not ready to settle down in a country I don't know and where I know no one. My home is here in the Congo, not in cold Switzerland. I hope we manage to sort this out soon.

I miss you lots and lots.

xxx Ta Juliette

'Those pictures she included, one of them is the one I showed you so many years ago in Brussels,' Max said.

The Green Elevator Cage

'They must be.'

Claudia leaned over to get closer to Max.

'I have to tell you something, I've never told anyone else.'

She took a sip of her cognac, as did Max.

'Ever since I can remember, I've had this recurring nightmare. I'm being dragged in the snow by my father who is holding my hand. We're walking very quickly. I'm holding your hand. We're running away from Africans. There are many of them. But you are only a little boy, your little legs can't keep up with us. The blacks eventually catch up with us and grab your other arm. They try to pull you away from me and I'm trying to hold on to my father's hand. He's strong and he's pulling me hard and going faster. I can feel that I'm losing you. I cry out to Father to slow down, but he keeps running faster. You cry out my name in desperation, but I can't hold on to you anymore. I let go of you. I cry. The Africans grab you, pick you up and run away with you. With your little arms stretched out, begging for me to come back, you cry out, "Claudia! Claudia!" You're crying desperately, but Father doesn't look back. I cry out, "They've taken Michel. Stop Father! Stop!" But he doesn't stop. And then I wake up. It's horrible Max! And it's each time the same thing. It never changes.'

She takes a sip of her cognac.

'And I feel so bad each time I wake up that I wasn't able to save you. That I let you go.'

'That's so distressing Claudia. I'm so sorry you have to live through these nightmares. How often do you have them?'

'It depends. Every six months, three months. It varies.'

'Is there something that triggers it?'

'No. Not really.'

'Have you seen a psychologist about this?'

'I have and they haven't been very helpful. They've even put me under hypnosis. But none of that has helped.'

Max takes a sip of his cognac.

'Let's read one more letter, the last one in the pile and see what it says,' Max said.

'Okay.'

Leopoldville, 15 April 1957

Dear Mammy,

This is a very difficult letter to write.

Hans and I are going to divorce. It has been on the cards for quite a while, but I didn't want to unnecessarily worry you. Soon after I got married five years ago, I knew I had made a terrible mistake. But I wanted to think that all would be okay. It wasn't Hans's fault. I simply wasn't ready to settle down. I was only 19. I have been unhappy for a long time Mammy. I couldn't yet commit to a permanent relationship. Hans being older was more mature than I was in that respect. And I hate to admit this, but I began to be unfaithful to my husband. I felt so bad because he was always good to me, but I couldn't find peace and happiness in our marriage.

Michel is not his child. The father is Michel Maréchal, a Swiss man who works with Hans. Complicating things is that Michel is now married, and I never told him that Michel is his son. But a few weeks ago, Hans and I had a big argument and in the heat of the war of words I told him that Michel was not his. But I didn't tell him that he's Michel's. It was horrible Mammy, horrible. I felt so, so bad. I begged for forgiveness. I wanted to turn the clock back, start from scratch, when things were beautiful, and we were in love. I felt so bad for what I had done to Hans, who didn't deserve this. He had always been good to me.

After the dust settled down, we agreed that it was best that we divorce rather than separate and hope to get back together later. There were too many other things that would make us getting back together unlikely. Next month, we will leave Leopoldville and go our separate ways. Hans will take Claudia and go to Zurich, and I will take Michel and come to Brussels. If it's okay with you, I'll stay with you for a short while until I decide what I'm going to do for the rest of my life! Hans has kindly offered to provide a small living allowance for Michel. This is what I mean by his kindness. He certainly has no obligation to do anything regarding Michel's well-being.

Mammy, I'm so distressed to know that I will no longer be able to see and hold to my heart my beautiful Claudia every day. I cry so much every day thinking about it. I'm so, so sad. But I know I brought it on to myself and I have absolutely no excuse. Claudia will pay the price for my selfishness. I just hope that when she's older she'll forgive me and understand what I'm going through.

I'm sorry to dump all this on you and I hope you will understand and forgive me for my big mistakes.

We haven't finalised the dates, but I should be in Brussels in about a month's time.

I love you so much.

xxx Ta Juliette

P.S. I'm sure happy Bonpa is no longer around to see this. It would have so saddened him.

'Poor Mum, she was so sad when she wrote that letter. You could almost touch her tears,' Claudia said.

'I know. I can't even start imagining the emotional pain she would have been going through thinking of not seeing you every day but only very rarely. I couldn't live with myself if I knew that I couldn't see Genevieve daily, especially when she was very young.'

'I know. It would have been horrible,' Claudia said.

'I know I've said this before, but I'm so sorry that you were separated from Mum like that so young and from me.'

'Thank you, Max. But that's a long time ago. And I've moved on. I had to.'

Silence.

'You know, what I simply could never understand is why she never wanted to talk about the past whenever we asked her,' Max said.

'I know. Maybe it's a generational thing. Remember that my father was the same.'

'I know. But Mum had it down to a fine art.'

'That's for sure.'

'I remember one day when I was walking with her in Brussels at the time of Mammy's funeral, pointing to a side street, she let slip out that she'd lived there in the late 1950s and early 1960s. I was so shocked to hear what she had so casually revealed. So, I asked her why was it that she was living in Brussels, but I wasn't with her but with Mammy instead.'

'What did she say?'

'She then realised that she shouldn't have mentioned what to her was just a minor detail. So, she just brushed off my question by mumbling something like, 'I don't know. It's so long ago. Who cares?' I told her I did, but she simply said, "Oh, don't worry about it. It's all in the past anyway." And so, once again, she shut down that conversation.'

'That's incredible Max. So, she really didn't want to have the responsibility of bringing up her child,' Claudia said.

'It looks like it, doesn't it?'

'I thought she was based in Luxembourg or some other country and that she would come and visit you when back from a trip.'

'So did I. But now it looks like it wasn't the case, or certainly not always. And again, that's what she let slip out by mistake. Who knows what other secrets are out there that we know nothing about?'

'I often wonder why she was like that, so secretive about things that affected our lives.'

'I know. Maybe it was living under German occupation during the war which affected her. I just don't know,' Max said. 'And even that she never really talked about.'

'Well, one thing is certain we'll never know why, nor know the whole truth.'

'Yep, that's for sure.'

Silence.

'And discovering that picture of Michel secretly tucked away deep in her wallet confirms again her total reluctance to talk about the past,' said Max.

'But also, how much that extra-marital liaison had affected her.'

'That's right.'

'It also shows how much Michel had meant to her,' Claudia said.

'Clearly, a lot,' Max said, 'to put it mildly.'

'Quite unbelievable, really.'

Silence.

'With all these letters, it almost slipped my mind. I've been meaning to suggest for quite a while now that we take a DNA test. I'd like to eliminate the possibility that we are after all full siblings. Mum may well have got it wrong,' Max said.

'Why do you think this now?' Claudia asked, looking slightly surprised.

'Actually, ever since I saw Michel in the home movie in Brussels, I've had doubts. He simply looks too dark, too tall for him to be my father. It's just a gut feeling.'

'I know what you mean.'

'This doesn't mean that Hans is my father. It could be someone else. Somebody we know nothing about, and Mum never told us.'

'Yes, that's true.'

'So, I'd really like to eliminate that possibility. Put my mind to rest.'

'Of course, I understand.'

'We can have the test done very easily and quickly tomorrow morning. They only need to take a swab of the inside of our mouths. Then they can send us the results back home. It's not at all expensive.'

'Okay, let's do it then. But don't expect a big revelation.'

'Of course, but let's just do it.'

'Okay, that's fine. I'll do that for my little brother,' Claudia said, smiling and holding Max's hand.

'That's great. Thank you.'

'I think we should go back to the hotel now. We've spent over three hours here. I'm surprised they haven't kicked us out.'

Max finished the little that remained of his cognac.

As Max was getting up, Claudia gently held back his arm, 'Max, it was great to be together tonight and just talk. Reading Mum's letters and talking about them was such a great way to almost have 'closure', as they say in America. She's never really told us how she felt about the divorce and so many other things. No matter how often we asked her.'

'I know. She simply wouldn't talk about it, but nor would Hans.'

'I know.'

'But that's the way it is. There's absolutely nothing we can do about it. But even with all these unanswered questions it meant a lot to me too to be here with you.'

'I'll be able to think about this adieu to Mum when I'm at my ten-day retreat in the mountains north of Zurich.'

'Is this one of the retreats you do on a regular basis?'

'Yes, I love it. I'll be going straight to it when I get back to Switzerland. I don't want to ruin the mood by stopping by the house first and talking to people.'

'Fair enough.'

'The people who run the retreat are so wonderful. And it's so peaceful and serene. It has large gardens, and you can just sit around read, go to some seminars, do some painting, whatever you want. The food is wholesome and it's good for your mind.'

'But do they make G&Ts?' Max asked with a big smile on his face.

'No.'

'In that case, it's not for me!'

'Now, you sound just like Mum and her dry martinis.'

'Quelle surprise!'

****

Canberra, 10 August 2019

Dearest Claudia,

I have just got back yesterday but I wanted to write you a letter while my trip to Florida was still fresh in my mind.

I hope your flight back to Switzerland was okay. At least it wasn't as long as mine back to Australia. When you read this letter, you will have had your 10 days at the retreat. I hope it was exactly what you wanted it to be - therapeutic.

I wanted to tell you how very special it had been for me that we could be together to say farewell to Mum. As a matter of fact, I'm writing this letter with Mum's fountain pen, the one she used for so many years writing us letters from around the world. I also wanted to let you know that I have forgiven Mum for the sadness she unwittingly inflicted on me when I was a little boy. I sincerely hope she rests in peace.

I was thinking of your recurrent nightmare that you told me about in Florida. I really hope that now that Mum has passed away and that we've read Mum's feelings about how she felt about the divorce and her painful separation from you, you will no longer have those nightmares. Obviously, in those nightmares you've been trying to correct what had happened so long ago.

I'd better let you go. I love this time of the year in Canberra. Many of the wattles are blooming and that means I have an ocean of yellowness in front of me. I planted every one of the wattle bushes and trees in my garden over many years. I know each one of them well; they are like my children! They attract the birds, so that's an additional bonus. I hope that one day you will come and visit, and I'll be able to show you around this beautiful country I've adopted as my home for almost forty years.

Let's talk soon.

Gros bisous xxx Max

P.S. I haven't received the DNA test results back yet. But I'm sure they will be arriving any day now.

Epilogue
(2019)

With trepidation, he opened the letter from the DNA Testing Clinic which arrived today. He opened it with the letter opener Mammy had bought him when he turned eighteen.

Fort Lauderdale, August 15, 2019

Dear Dr Van Den Berghe,

On August 10, 2019, Ms Claudia Sigrist and you requested we conduct a sibling DNA test.

We conducted the relevant tests on your respective DNA samples, and we can confirm that your DNA match.

Accordingly, we can confirm with 99.9% certainty that you and Claudia are <u>full siblings</u>.

As a matter of information, all our results have been upheld whenever these have been challenged in a court of law.

We have sent a similar letter to Ms Claudia Sigrist.

Thank you for availing yourselves of our services.

Yours sincerely,

Management (signed)
DNA Testing Clinic

He re-read the short letter three times.

He was sitting in his study. The sun was starting to go down, its rays filtered through the numerous wattle flowers in his garden. He looked up and stared outside, dazed, completely stunned. A magpie landed on the birdbath just outside his window. Its mate joined him, and in unison, they made that wonderful corralling sound of contentment and ownership.

He looked at the calendar. Claudia would only be back from her retreat tomorrow. The DNA letter would be waiting for her, he thought.

He went to the large wooden cabinet and took out his old tin box with King Baudouin and Queen Fabiola on the lid. He opened it and put the letter in it on top of Claudia's lighter. He put the lid back on and returned the tin box to its rightful place next to his many stamp albums which included his very first one given to him by Uncle Pierre.

Jane called out, 'Dinner is ready, darling.'

'I'll be right there.'

He looked out of the window again. The magpies had been replaced by a large sulphur-crested cockatoo at the birdbath. The sun was fast setting, with the shadow of the massive gum tree now covering much of the garden.

He looked at the framed picture of his mother on his desk. She would have been in her late twenties in that picture, he thought, the way he remembered her as a little boy in Brussels each time she would come out of the green elevator cage to visit him.

He lifted the framed picture to his lips, and he kissed the picture.

'Rest in Peace, Mum.'

Max left the study.

About the Author

Born in the then Belgian Congo, Claude Rakisits grew up in Brussels and, later, in the Middle East, Africa and North America. Thanks to an adventurous aviator stepfather, Claude discovered exotic lands and fascinating people. From New York, he flew to Australia on a scholarship in July 1982 to undertake a PhD in Political Science at the University of Queensland. Liking Australia so much he decided to call Australia home, cashed in his return ticket and handed back his Green Card to an astonished American consul, and never looked back. He has worked on national security issues for the Australian government and as an adviser to senior Australian politicians. Affiliated with Australian and overseas academic institutions and think tanks, he continues to write and speak on international affairs while also writing fiction. Dr Rakisits is married with an adult daughter. He divides his time between Australia and Europe. This is his first novel.

*Available worldwide from Amazon
and all good bookstores*

Michael Terence Publishing

www.mtp.agency

mtp.agency

@mtp_agency